There Are No Do-Overs at
RETIREMENT

A 10 Day Financial Blueprint to Boost Your Retirement Confidence

SUNWOOK JIN, CFP®, CRPC®, CMFC®, EA

ISBN-13: 978-1497446427

Book Cover & Design by PIXEL eMarketing INC.

Legal Disclaimer

Dedicated

*To My Parents, Byong-Hwa & Myong-Suk Jin,
who left their livelihood in South Korea for a better
opportunity for me and my brother.*

*To My Wife, Erica, who makes everything
possible. I appreciate you.*

To my clients:

*Thank you for your trust and confidence in
my ability to help you achieve your goals and dreams.*

Contents

Building Your Financial Blueprint

There comes a time in every couple's relationship when you have to sit down and start planning for the future. When this happens, it will benefit you both to invest some time and effort in creating a solid financial blueprint.

This blueprint will make sure that when the time comes and you have reached your twilight years, you and your spouse are able to retire at the right time with enough money to keep you comfortable and financially secure until the very end.

Nobody likes to talk about a time when you will be older, but that time is coming—you can count on that. The key difference between couples that retire happy and those that are unable or unsuited for retirement is early blueprint planning.

What you are about to do with this 10-day guide to building your financial blueprint is to guarantee that your financial health is adequate when you and your spouse are too old to work, struggle, and scrimp for money.

As a financial consultant and retirement planner, I have helped hundreds of married couples make the awkward transition to beginning their dynamic careers to planning for the day when those careers come to an end.

You may still have plans to make a lot of money in your life, to travel, and to have enough by the time that you retire. Take it from me; this does not always go as planned. Too often people start planning their retirement late, which results in financial complications, working well into their old age, or never having the opportunity to retire at all.

This carefully structured financial blueprint will help you get the most out of boring and complicated financial terms, action plans, and goals so that you and your spouse know from today that—when the time comes—you will be financially able to retire and retire happy.

Spend some time working through this easy-to-use guide, and start structuring your sound retirement right now. The future version of yourself will look back and be pleased that you did.

CHAPTER 1

The Basics of Retirement Planning

"Preparation for old age should begin no later than one's teens. A life which is empty of purpose until 65 will not suddenly become filled on retirement."

DWIGHT L. MOODY

Welcome to the 10-day retirement guide, where you will find out what you need to organize in order to get your financial affairs in order for your retirement. You already know that one day you are going to wake up and be at the right age for it.

Your job right now is to hone in on those little financial matters that will make retirement not just possible but an absolute pleasure. A crisis is coming for couples that do not plan ahead, and I would encourage you to not be a part of this crisis by starting today.

What Are Your Retirement Income Needs?

It is day one of your 10-day retirement planning expedition. I have broken it down for you so that you and your spouse can sit together after work for the next 10 days to get all of this organized and sorted for the rest of your life.

The very first thing that you need to do is understand that when you get older, your income needs may be greater than they are now. The world will definitely be different, and who knows how much more of an impact financial markets, inflation, and your dollar will be worth in 30 or so years.

That is why you need to find out what your retirement income needs will be and also why it is not an easy question to answer. Typically, and as a rule, you should keep an eye on your decisions moving forward. You can always change your blueprint down the line.

Retirement planning is not an exact science, but there are many techniques (formula based) that will help you determine a number that you can then work towards. Once you have that definable number, you can start planning for it.

Any number of factors can influence this number. Start with these core questions:

- How do I envision my lifestyle once I retire?
- At what age do I want to stop working? (It does not mean that you will retire at a certain age. However, the key is when you would want to retire without financial worries.)
- If I had complete financial security, how would I spend my time?
- Will my hobbies increase my overall budget?
- Do I want to travel during retirement years? If so, what will these expenses cost today?
- Do I want to leave any legacy to my kids, grandkids, etc.?

Based on what I described above, and if the retirement date was today, how much income would I need every month/year?

Key information for you to consider:

- Many of my fellow financial professional colleagues may say that you need to replace 75–90% of your current income. I agree, if you decide to continue living your current lifestyle. However, YOU may envision your lifestyle at retirement to be even better than your working years. (And this may cost you more than your current income.) So it could be much higher than a 100% replacement.
- Life expectancy: No one really knows this answer. But the last thing you want to happen is to outlive your assets.

How to Calculate the Gap!

Once you have the basics of all of these questions answered, there is one more thing to consider here—the gap! I want to be honest with you so that your retirement planning goes as well as expected.

You do not want to end up short in your old age. I have seen it happen, and it is just about the worst thing you can imagine. Most retirement planners need to take the gap into account. So...what is the gap?

The gap can be defined as the path that you are on right now—and your eventual desired trajectory. This is the gap. In order to close this gap, you need to know where your savings are right now and where they need to be.

Having a gap in your retirement savings can leave you with a less-than-suitable income when you are older. It is best to prepare for this gap so that it is as small (or non- existent) as possible. What you have now will almost certainly not last.

To calculate what your gap will be, use a simple retirement gap calculator. These can be found online, or you can choose to work it out together based on this formula. This equation helps you to understand that you may be retired for 20 or more years.

This is an essential part of figuring out how much money you will need for retirement:

- If you have determined that to meet your retirement needs you will require some $71,000 gross income a year, you need to subtract this from Social Security.
- If the Social Security on that is $21,000–$71,000 in gross income, you are left with $50,000 per year of income.
- You need to invest enough money to generate this $50,000 a year in income. It depends on your rate of return and whether you will spend/not spend your principal.

- If you are getting a rate of return at 5% per annum, you need more than a million bucks to generate that $50,000 per year of income. Some 25 years later, you should still have that $1 million.

- The calculation looks like this: $1,000,000 x 5% = $50,000. If you want to spend your principal amount (the million), you will need $704,000 in earnings at 5% a year to last for 25 years. At the end of those years, all the money will be gone.

Warning:

This is before calculating inflation and taxes. You must consider the cost of goods/services going up every year and your silent partner, Uncle Sam. Therefore, you actually need more than $704,000.

Here is an example of someone retiring today who needs $50,000 per year (after tax), and you anticipate the cost of goods/services to go up by 3.75% per year and assume you pay 20% for taxes for 25 years of retirement.

So in this example, you need more than $1.35 million to retire TODAY.

Based on the sample above, the target asset goal depends on how many years you have before you retire.

This Is How Much You Need to Save

No one knows how much you should save until you know how much you need to have for retirement, because it differs from person to person. Starting out, the goal is to aim for a number that will keep you comfortable, maintain your quality of life, and be as high as possible.

I know a lot of retirement planners who argue that their clients should save 10–15% of their income from their early twenties. This is an ideal situation but not always the case in this modern age. People are planning for retirement later and later—in their thirties and even later.

The general rule is that you will need between 25 and 30 dollars in savings to cover every dollar of the annual shortfall between your income and expenses. If your retirement expenses exceed your Social Security and pension by $20,000 a year, you will need a gap nest egg.

This nest egg is a savings of between $500,000 and $600,000. It is no small amount of savings, that is for sure! It takes discipline and effort to put money away for you and your spouse later on in life, but it is essential that you do it now.

Your retirement savings will be used to cover that gap we were talking about on the previous page. This is a lump sum amount that will yield the annual retirement income that you need to maintain financial balance.

Everyone will want to save different amounts according to their careers, interests, and quality of life. The trick is to figure out what you need and then work from there. You never want to dip below what you will need in order to have a successful retirement.

The baby boomer generation fell short on their retirement needs by $400,000. As a result, they are now forced to live in greatly reduced financial situations to survive. Experts predict that Gen X and Ys like you will do even worse than that.

So calculate the savings that you need, and take your gap into account. Then make a plan to get that savings started. It may be the one thing (outside of your pension) that will make up whatever financial shortfall may come when you reach your twilight years.

Building Retirement Fund Power

If you are spending most of your paycheck and saving 10% of it every month, then chances are the 80% income replacement rule will help you retire at 65. The more you save, the better off you will be. That is just common sense!

Another more "common sense" method of approaching retirement is to create your very own retirement plan. That is what this book is for. Building retirement fund power means making your financial situation idyllic over the course of your life.

- Make sure that you pay off all the debt that you have. Debt is for people that love to struggle with cash flow.

- Invest in a quality retirement fund, such as a 401k or Roth IRA. These will help you save consistently, and that can be a powerful motivator.

- Continue to grow your net worth until you reach a comfortable number that allows you to earn income and live off that percentage of income later in life.

- Look at converting your taxable portfolio into either tax-deferred or tax-free. Many people are choosing to take some of their saved money and invest it later in life so that the income generated by this investment increases their nest egg and makes up for any gap or shortfall.

Social Security and/or your employer-sponsored pension plan may likely NOT be enough for you to retire on by the time you reach your older years. Building fund power is a must if you are going to retire happy.

Learning how to work with these retirement funds, where to invest, and how to save and improve your income overall will do a lot in helping you retire when you reach your chosen age.

Adding retirement funds to your overall retirement plan will give you access to an additional source of income above and beyond your company's pension and Social Security.

The Investment Options That Count

There are quite literally dozens of great investment options that will count towards your overall retirement portfolio, which is key to building a quality retirement blueprint. These options will help you see that you have a lot of choice (and risk) when assembling your retirement plan. Here are some samples:

- Individual Retirement Accounts, or IRAs, are popular because they earn funds for you in retirement. In this book, we will go through traditional IRAs and Roth IRAs. Popular investments in these retirement plans are Stocks, Bonds, Mutual Funds, and Exchange Traded Funds (ETFs) to name a few.

- Annuities allow you to invest lump sums or small payments over time into a future pay out stream for life or for a certain period. We will go over them later.

- Mutual funds are another popular one that are made up of a simple pool of funds collected from many investors. It is managed by professionals, and they may invest in stocks, bonds, and other investment vehicles based on its investment objectives.

- A Certificate of Deposit is a low risk option that provides you with a higher rate of interest because you do not need access to your funds.

- The return is guaranteed when the CD is held to maturity, and the interest rates are better than checking account or savings rates. Generally, longer term CDs offer higher rates than shorter term CDs.

- You can also try hand picking individual stocks if you have an appetite for being more aggressive with your investments. This does take some effort in research and monitoring on your part. However, if you are just starting out, you may not want to go with this route.

- Individual Bonds are a great source of income. Bonds are simply lending your money to a corporation, government, or non-profit institution for a certain period of time, and then they pay you the interest only until it matures.

- Online banks and credit unions offer higher yields than traditional banks, so moving your liquid assets there could make a difference.

The Right Tools for the Job

Reliable retirement planning, as you can see, varies because YOU, as the person retiring, really have to set the boundaries for all the formulas that need to be calculated.

As a married couple, you will be dealing with one, perhaps two income streams and dozens of options. These choices will literally determine whether or not you are able to comfortably retire one day.

That is why you need the right tools for the job. The right tools include knowing and understanding what ALL of your options are and how they will affect you as time marches by. It also includes knowing who to trust and why and when to become alarmed if things are not going according to plan.

Retirement planning cannot be done alone. You may want an advisor or a coach to help you. These are turbulent financial seas we are navigating here! I really believe that with enough guidance and explanation, you can start to make the right decisions about your money so that when retirement happens, it is a smooth and pleasurable transition.

If you did not quite understand the concepts and ideas that I have spoken about thus far, that is okay! The first day is always the most confusing. In this book, I will walk you through all of it again so that step by step, you can see what would be best for your family.

From determining your income needs to saving, creating retirement plans, and investing—I will take you through each day so that you are never caught out with any retirement planning jargon or strategy.

This is your life, and you deserve to know how to plan for the end of it. My aim is not only to teach you about how but why and to provide you with the best chance that you have of exploding your income enough to have an amazing retirement.

CHAPTER 2

Determining Your Retirement Income Needs

"Retirement at 65 is ridiculous.
When I was 65 I still had pimples."

GEORGE BURNS

I like to think of a retirement blueprint like the blueprints that you need when building a house from scratch. You may have a general idea of what you want that house to look like, but without the right tools, advice, and processes, it can turn into a disaster.

A good retirement blueprint is detailed, clear, and to the point. That is why we are going to start at the beginning again—to move through each process slowly and carefully so that you can fully understand your options.

The Income Starting Point

It is day two, and so far all you have understood is that you have a lot more to understand in the upcoming nine days of this blueprint plan. That is okay! No one starts off with a total understanding of retirement.

Step one on day two is breaking down your retirement income needs. It is true that you need to know what is coming in (or going to come in) so that you can nail down the numbers you need for those calculations.

An "income-replacement" rate is used to help you calculate how MUCH of your current salary you will need after you retire. By establishing what this number is, you can attempt to set a standard of living for yourself in old age.

- *How much do you earn every month? Write down the number.*

As I mentioned earlier, the rule of thumb is that you will need some 75–90% of your current salary from a variety of sources (personal retirement assets like 401k, Social Security, and investments) in order to maintain your current quality of life.

Then there are some experts saying that 135% is the more realistic figure. It takes more of those pesky factors into account, such as market inflation. To even this out, answer the question:

- *How much do you want to earn in retirement?*

Now you have two numbers: your income and your desired retirement income.

Retirement Expense Projection: The Rules

What do you think your expenses will look like in 30 years? The answer to that question is that you just do not know. Ten years ago you did not have a smartphone expense, and now you do. In the age of technology, you may be paying off a flying car in 30 years.

But back to reality. You need to project what your retirement expenses will be. To do this, you need a firm understanding that your needs will be greater (not less) when you are older.

Here are the rules:

- Your goal is to lessen all of your debt or eliminate it completely before you retire. This will alleviate some financial pressure on you.

- Write down each and every one of your expenses that you have today. Include things such as hobbies, traveling, charitable giving, etc.

- You must take into account the best possible level of healthcare for you and your spouse. Anything can happen, and it generally does. Medical expenses can bankrupt a family in a few short months. Prepare for that.

Answer these important questions (in today's $):

- What will your housing expenses be?
- What will your food expenses be?
- What will your transportation expenses be?
- What will your healthcare expenses be? (Very important)
- What will your clothing and personal item expenses be?
- What will your travel expenses be?
- What will your entertainment expenses look like?
- What other expenses can you foresee having?

From this exercise, you should have a ballpark number, a general idea of what a good life will cost you 30 years from now. This is just a projection, but it gives you a starting point. You will need this starting point if you are going to prepare for comfortable retirement.

When Will You Retire?

Now that you know what you earn, how much you will need to earn, and what your expenses will be, you can focus on the most uncomfortable question of them all.

- *When will you retire? Write it down.*

Remember that when you quit your job, your earnings cease and desist. Then it is just you and your retirement plan. You have to be able to AFFORD to quit your job and financially move into a comfortable retirement.

In order to decide at what age to retire, consider this—some people retire at 40. Some at 50. Some retire after they have hit it big at the casino in their 30s. Most people, however, will retire at 65 and older. This is when retirement needs to take over.

- Take into account that pensions and/or Social Security may not be enough.

- The question for retirement is always going to be—do you have enough money to retire? You should know this well in advance for your own peace of mind.

- What do you want to do with the money you have earned? If your dream is to travel around the world or invest in something close to your heart (such as a charity), then make sure that you can afford it.

- Are you psychologically ready to retire? The term "retirement" does not have to mean that you stop working. Many people continue to work until they pass away. They love working! If you love your job, retirement will be strictly financial. That way if anything happens and you cannot work, you can still enjoy your life.

Take a few minutes to discuss the ages of retirement with your spouse. You should both write down on a piece of paper what those ages will be. Make sure that you take each other's ages into account too.

Estimating Your Life Expectancy

Another number to add to your formula list is the age that you will live to. This is the most disturbing figure of all but a necessary one that you need.

First of all, there are government life expectancy calculators that you can find online that will ask you for your general age and gender. It will give you a number. This is a number that you can work from—taking into account your lifestyle, occupation, and various other things.

Grab your life expectancy off one of these sites. Write it down.

Life expectancy is calculated based on how old you are now, less the projected national estimated total years the average person lives. A 31-year-old male, for example, will live for another 50 years, according to their life expectancy.

82 – 31.1 = 50.9 (months included). You will need these numbers from both of you.

A better way to personalize this population number is this. How old is the oldest person that you have known from your family of your own gender? Write down the number. It is more representative of what you may live to if you do not pass in an accident or from disease.

Your life expectancy can easily increase if you are very healthy and active. It can also decrease if you are unhealthy and exhibit risky behaviors. But these are all variables that no one in the financial industry can measure—so we use the ones mentioned previously.

To be safe, any projected years after the retiring age of 60–65 are seen as years that you need to prepare for. This can be as long as 20–30 years. That means that you need to prepare for a life without "earned" income for as long as that.

How to Identify Your Retirement Income Sources

The next step in day two is about understanding where your retirement income is going to come from. I am going to assume that you do not have many or any of them just yet, as you are just beginning to orientate yourself in serious retirement planning.

Identify where your retirement income sources will come from. These can be from anywhere, including:

- *Retirement accounts*: Put together your 401k and IRAs now so that you can defer taxes on retirement savings and investment earnings.
- *Savings accounts and CDs*: A savings lump sum can be a great way of bridging any financial gaps. Many retirees keep a year or more's worth of income in a fixed account.

- *Social Security*: You will receive monthly payments from the Social Security Administration, which will keep up with inflation. The age at which you start to collect it, however, determines how much it will be.

- *Roth IRAs*: Pre-pay your income tax on some of your retirement savings with the Roth IRA. Contributions that are made with already taxed dollars after the age of 59 and a half are tax free.

- *Stocks and mutual funds*: Stock market trading can grow your portfolio with guidance from the right broker. It helps your money keep up with inflation.

- *Your company's pension*: Pensions are offered by some companies. Today, more and more companies are not offering this anymore.

- *Bonds*: A fairly good source of income with limited loss potential makes bonds a good investment for risk-sensitive investors.

- *Your home equity*: Make sure that your mortgage is already paid off so that you have fast access to a loan or reverse mortgage if you need it.

- *Health insurance*: Your health insurance is a critical part of your retirement plan specifically because age can lead to so much medical cost.

Dealing with Income Shortfall

It can cost big bucks to fill a shortfall when you realize that you have one post retirement. It is far better to plan for a shortfall so that when you get there, you do not have to worry about living with one.

The question then becomes—how do you and your spouse deal with a retirement income shortfall? The younger you are the better because it gives you more time to make up the amount that you will lack later.

- Consider your projected lifestyle.
- Consider that economic climates will change, resulting in shortfall.
- Consider that planning to be short is SMART financially.

There are a number of ways to deal with shortfall. Here they are:

- Work for longer. Retire from your job, then do something else that brings in a solid income. Plan for this!
- When you bring in another income, you can claim your Social Security benefit later—which means that you will receive a higher monthly payment.
- Spend less, save more! Cliché as it sounds, the only way to make up a deficit is by saving more and spending less now when you are young. Maybe you should increase the project monthly target that you want to reach for old age.
- Refinance your home mortgage if your interest rate has dropped since taking out the loan for your home. (You will save!)
- Scale down, and move to a less expensive property where maintenance and access is easier.
- If you have two cars, plan to have one good enough to sell for a nice price. You can manage with one car between two people in retirement.
- Reduce expenses related to entertainment, and take advantage of all pensioner discounts and benefits that you can find.

My favorite way to recover from shortfall is to plan for it right now. Expect to be short of money and to work harder to put away more or to create investments that will generate greater income opportunities for you.

CHAPTER 3

How to Save for Retirement

"I love the Roth IRA. Tax-free income
in retirement is a truly great deal."

SUZE ORMAN

It is day three, which means that it is time to get serious about your retirement savings. How do you save for retirement anyway? Are there really that many options? The answer to that question is yes! You need to know which ones will work for you.

In this chapter, I will be working through the various financial plans that you can put in place in order to diversify your retirement income so that you have enough money in your twilight years. That, after all, is why you are doing this!

Working with Sponsored Retirement Plans

The first thing to investigate is your employer-sponsored retirement plan. This is when your employer automatically deducts an amount from your paycheck to be paid into a retirement plan of your choosing.

They are beneficial for obvious reasons—you do not even realize that you are saving for them. You decide how much to dedicate to that plan, up to the defined limit. You can also change this contribution amount on certain days of the year.

There are many different types of employer-sponsored retirement plans. They are the 401k, 403b, 457b, SARSEPs, and SIMPLE plans you come across most often.

Your employer may decide to match some or all of your contributions up to a certain point. This is only if you have met certain criteria set by your employer.

One of the most popular ways to save for retirement is with your 401k or similar because it is so easy to sign up, and it can be deducted from your pay automatically. However, you still assume the risk of how aggressive or conservative your investments are. When the time comes, you could have a nice payout. The questions is, should you use this tactic?

Find out if you are able to participate in your company's 401k or equivalent where you work. Then, find out if they match. If they do, you should contribute to max out the matching contribution. (Personally, you MUST!). *For example*: If your company matches $1 for $1 for up to 3% of your income, you should contribute at least 3% of your income to maximize this benefit.

Also make a point of understanding your options if you ever have to leave that employer. You have four options:

First, leave it at your old plan. Second, transfer to your new 401k plan. Third, roll it over to your existing IRA/Roth IRA. Fourth, cash it in, and contribute to a Roth IRA.

The next type of retirement savings tool is a Roth IRA. As I mentioned before, IRA stands for "individual retirement account" and is used by many people as an additional way of saving for their golden years.

In a Roth IRA, your money actually grows tax-free—which is excellent news. You may be able to contribute up to $5,500 per person (additional $1,000 if you are 50 or older).

It is also way more flexible than a 401k because you can invest that money wherever you like—in real estate or in bonds or mutual funds. There is a limit on how much you can contribute to your Roth IRA each year, so find out what that is.

- You or your spouse must have "eligible" earned income to contribute to a Roth IRA.
- When you contribute money to a Roth IRA, it continues to grow whether you put money in it or not.

- You can take out your Roth IRA at 59 ½ or later at any time, tax-free with no penalties.
- You can also take out your contributions before 59 ½ at any time.
- The Roth IRA therefore becomes an indispensable vehicle if you are eligible to participate.

If you save $5,500 per year and you earn 9% per year for the next 30 years, the accumulated value is $817,163. And it is tax-free. It will definitely make a difference when you retire.

Find out more about Roth IRAs and how you can get one going for each of you. Contributing to a Roth IRA is an excellent savings technique for retirement.

Again, to recap, tax-free growth and tax-free withdrawals—plus it can be put to good use making up for retirement gaps and eliminates any future tax.

Contributing to a Traditional IRA

Individual retirement accounts are great tools, as we have established. The next investment opportunity comes from a traditional IRA, which is slightly different from a Roth IRA.

Your traditional IRA contributions may be deducted from your taxable income, and your earnings may grow tax-deferred until you withdraw them in retirement. Retirees often find themselves in a lower tax bracket than in pre-retirement, so tax-deferred means the money will be taxed at a lower rate.

- Traditional IRAs and Roth IRAs both grow tax-deferred. However, the traditional IRAs do not allow for tax-free distribution at retirement.
- You may only have a traditional IRA or Roth IRA if you do not have an employer-sponsored retirement plan.

- Annually, you can contribute $5,500 to your IRA. If you are married, as a couple, you can contribute $11,000, which makes it better.

- Any contributions that you make may be tax deductible up to the entire 100% (traditional IRA only).

There are several key benefits here, namely the tax deductions and no income limits on participation in the plan. You may not be eligible to receive tax deductions, but you are eligible to contribute to a traditional IRA on a non-deductible basis.

If you are able to deduct the contributions into a traditional IRA, this in turn lowers your tax liability quite a bit. Any funds that you withdraw as an older individual will probably be subject to lower taxes. These plans work well with several other retirement plans and fit neatly into a retirement blueprint.

If you happen to pass away, the money will become available to your kids or family.

The Annuity Options

An annuity is a product that you purchase through an insurance company. It will pay out income on a month by month basis and can be used as part of your retirement strategy. If you are looking for a steady stream of income after you have retired, these annuities are a great strategy.

Basically, you invest in the annuity now (you buy it) and then it will pay out to you in the future. Receiving income from an annuity can happen however you like: monthly, quarterly, or annually. You could even withdraw all of the value at once. You can choose to receive payments from your annuity for the rest of your life or for several years.

There are four main types of annuities (we will discuss in more detail later):

- *Immediate Annuities*: Once you have bought one, you will receive payments soon afterwards. It is instant. You could purchase from one or multiple insurance companies.
- *Fixed Annuities*: It issues a guaranteed or a minimum rate of interest on your investment.
- *Variable Annuities*: These are ideal for someone looking for a stock market-like return. However, you assume all the risk of gain and loss of return.
- *Equity-Indexed Annuities*: This is a combination of a guaranteed return with some upside.

Life Insurance and Deferred Compensation

You can fund your retirement using a life insurance plan; the question is—should you? It is true that you could access life insurance's cash value tax-free. However, often insurance agents will make it seem like investing in a life insurance policy is the best thing ever. You must understand the ins and outs.

Life insurance should be used as a life insurance. When you need a roof over your head, you may decide to either rent or buy a home. Not all situations call for everyone to buy a home instead of renting for a short period of time.

Life insurance can be used to supplement your retirement income. Just know that not all situations call for you to buy the most expensive plan.

As for deferred compensation plans, these are also employer-sponsored. The 457b is a prime example of a deferred compensation plan. As usual, your employer will deduct an amount off your salary and put it into an account for you. This money is then tax-deferred. It can help you bridge the gap in your Social Security and pension plans.

Your job is to find out about the life insurance and deferred compensation plans where you work. Familiarize yourself with them, and know what you are signing.

Check on the fees for having the account, the tax benefits, and when you can access the funds that you are putting away. These are all important factors when working with deferred compensation plans.

Alert! Be aware that if your employer ever goes bankrupt, their creditors are entitled to your deferred compensation plan. You do not have any control over this, so it is a risky plan to put into place because there is no guarantee that you will ever receive that money.

Mutual Funds

When it comes to mutual funds, there are many options. The average retirement portfolio will have a mix of stocks, cash, and bonds that will be used to supply them with cash when the owners are retired.

There are thousands of mutual funds to invest in. The important thing is that you diversify so that you have a greater chance of success. You can also outright buy a fund that invests in stocks, bonds, and cash all at once.

These life-cycle funds are broken down into size, type, region, and sector. They all matter when you are investing your money in such a risky field. A professional fund manager that knows their job can get excellent returns for you. They decide when to buy and sell your funds and are directly responsible for making you money.

CHAPTER 4

Your Retirement Plan

"Sadly, retirement planning, in many circumstances, has become nothing more than planned procrastination."

RICHIE NORTON

Day 4 has arrived, which means that it is time to get into the serious business of creating your couple's retirement plan. Today is all about IRAs and Roth IRAs and how they can be used to help you prepare for the end of your working days.

In this chapter, I am going to take you through the various types of IRAs so that you can learn what they are and why you need to select one to add to your retirement portfolio.

Defining Traditional IRAs

A traditional IRA or traditional "individual retirement account" is really a retirement savings plan that has the potential to offer you beneficial tax breaks. As a financial advisor, I never feel secure until I have fully briefed my clients about these powerful savings tools and how they can supplement any existing 401k or other work-based plan.

There are two main types of IRA: traditional and Roth. In this section, I will cover both, but let's begin with the first kind: traditional. Almost anyone can opt to open a traditional IRA that they will then contribute to over time.

There are two main restrictions when you contribute:

1. You must be under age 70½ at the end of the year.

2. You must have taxable compensation, such as wages, salaries, commissions, tips, bonuses, or net income from self-employment. Taxable alimony and separate maintenance payments received by an individual are treated as compensation for IRA purposes. Compensation does not include earnings and profits from property, such as rental income, interest and dividend income, or any amount received as pension or annuity income or as deferred compensation.

If your taxes are less than your maximum contribution, you can only add in what you have paid in taxes. That is the catch! Any contributions that you make could be tax deductible on your federal income tax form.

Depending on your 401k status—and your spouse's status—you may be able to deduct all or part of your taxes from your traditional IRA. Once you hit age 70½, you must take the required minimum distribution (RMD) from your IRA.

From that point, you have to do this once a year until it runs out or you pass away. The fund allows you to draw more if you need it, but if you draw less than your RMD for the year, then you get stuck with a 50% penalty. It is in your best interest to draw the full amount every year.

The Benefits and Trade Offs of Traditional IRAs

Traditional IRAs are the most basic kind, and they are the bread and butter of retirement savings in most American homes. These plans have both positive and negative features, so let's go over them before you consider this kind of IRA as an option.

The Positive Features:

- The most obvious pro is that with the traditional IRA, you may be able to deduct your contribution from your income tax. You will pay a lower tax rate in retirement thanks to this contribution, which is great for your family.

- The tax claim is an "adjustment to income" claim, which means that you do not have to itemize. As long as you stick to the rules, you will benefit from it in retirement.
- Another great benefit is that when your money is in your traditional IRA, you do not have to pay any taxes on the growth. If one of your stocks goes nuts and makes you a fortune, guess what? No taxes on any gains! That means that you can reinvest the whole amount to quickly grow your fund balance.

The Trade Offs:

- If you are already covered by an employer-sponsored plan, then your ability to deduct contributions may be reduced or eliminated depending on your circumstances.
- If you withdraw funds from your traditional IRA, that same year you will have to pay tax on it, including deductible contributions and investment earnings.
- When you hit age 70½, as I mentioned before, you have to start taking your Required Minimum Distribution (RMD) every year. You can do this simply once a year or throughout the year.
- Any withdrawals taken before the age of 59½ may be subject to a 10% premature distribution penalty tax. In certain special circumstances, this penalty could be waived under a qualified distribution event.
- Finally, you pay taxes on your distribution at regular (ordinary) income rate, even if your funds represent long-term capital gains or dividends paid on investments held within your IRA.

**Warning: We simply do not know what the tax rate might be in the future when you decide to make your distribution. Therefore, future tax law could be dramatically different than today.

Defining Roth IRAs

A Roth IRA is the second kind of IRA that you could choose to invest in for retirement. It is an individual plan that offers nice tax benefits (like the traditional version) to encourage saving for retirement.

You can contribute up to $5,500.00 to your fund or 100% of your taxable compensation to your Roth IRA. People older than 50 can implement a "catch-up" contribution of up to $1,000.00 extra per year.

Your contributions to your Roth IRA will not be tax deductible, BUT your funds will grow tax deferred, and distributions are TAX-FREE under certain conditions—which can be very beneficial.

As a financial advisor, tax-free income in retirement is a big plus and something that you and your spouse should seriously consider. Your tax bracket does matter—both now and when you eventually retire—so keep that in mind.

Following the rules with your Roth IRA is important because this is what will get you that no up-front tax deduction. Every last cent that you stash in your Roth IRA belongs to you, which means that you can tap your contributions any time—tax and penalty free.

Contribution Limitations:

- *Single / Head of Household*: If your Modified Adjusted Gross Income (MAGI) for 2014 is $114,000 or less, you could make a full contribution to your Roth IRA. However, if your MAGI is between $114,000 and $129,000, you could make a reduced contribution. If your MAGI is over $129,000, you cannot make any contributions.

- *Married Filing Jointly*: If your MAGI for 2014 is $181,000 or less, you could make a full contribution to your Roth IRA. However, if your MAGI is between $181,000 and $191,000, you could make a reduced contribution. If your MAGI is over

$191,000, you cannot make any contributions.

- *Married Filing Separately*: If your MAGI is more than $10,000, you cannot make any contributions.

The Benefits and Trade Offs of Roth IRAs

There are many pros and cons involved when you decide to take out a Roth IRA. For couples, this IRA may make more sense because it gives you greater control over your fund distribution, which is always nice. Let's see why this is an option.

The Positive Features:

- You can continue to contribute to your account after the age of 70½ as long as you have a taxable compensation. This is preferable for people who intend to work into their 70s and beyond.
- All qualified distributions are 100% TAX-FREE. This, of all the benefits, makes using a Roth IRA a prominent choice.
- Unlike a traditional IRA, there is no Required Minimum Distribution (RMD) when you turn age 70½.
- A Roth IRA gives you flexibility to withdraw your contributions at any time before age 59½ without a penalty tax. That means that money is not fixed and stagnant; it can be used as you see fit.
- You can contribute to your Roth IRA even if you have an employer-sponsored retirement plan, and IRAs are notoriously broad when it comes to your range of investment choices.

The Trade Offs:

- Every contribution that you make is independent; it does not result in a tax deduction like the traditional IRA does.
- If your withdrawal does not qualify you for tax-free status, then that earning portion will be taxed by the federal government. There may even be withdrawal penalties if you

are under the age of 59½.

- There are special provisions that could apply to your Roth IRA if the fund has been converted or rolled over from a traditional IRA, simple IRA, or SEP IRA.

Comparing Traditional and Roth IRAs

At this point, your head is full of questions, and that is fine! Both traditional and Roth IRAs are different, and you would need each under certain circumstances. To make it easier for you to decide on which one you need, here is a comparison.

Traditional IRAs:

- The maximum annual contribution for traditional IRAs is less than $5,500.00 or 100% of earned income, or $6,500.00 if you are 50 or older.
- There are no income limitations for contributions.
- There are fully tax-deductible contributions if neither of you are covered by an employer retirement plan. If you are, your deduction depends on your filing status and income.
- There are age restrictions on contributions; for example, you cannot make annual contributions when you hit 70 and a half.
- Traditional IRAs have tax-deferred growth.
- There are required minimum distributions during your lifetime. They must begin by April 1st the following year as you reach age 70 and a half.
- There is federal income tax on distributions to the extent that a distribution represents deductible contributions and investment earnings.
- There is a 10% penalty on early distributions. The penalty applies to taxable distributions if you are under 59 and a half and do not qualify for an exception.

- The beneficiaries pay income tax on distributions after the IRA owner's death to the extent that a distribution represents deductible contributions and investment earnings.

Roth IRAs:

- The maximum annual contribution for Roth IRAs is less than $5,500.00 or 100% of earned income, or $6,500.00 if you are 50 or older.
- There are income limitations for contributions.
- You have no tax-deductible contributions to a Roth IRA.
- There are no age restrictions on contributions.
- Roth IRAs have tax-deferred growth; it is tax-free if you meet all of the requirements for qualified distribution.
- There are no required distributions during your lifetime.
- There are no taxes on qualified distributions. For nonqualified distributions, only the earnings portion is taxable.
- There are no penalties for qualified distributions. For nonqualified distributions, the penalty may apply to the earnings portion, but there are special rules. Ask your financial advisor about it.
- It is includable in taxable estate of IRA owner at their death.
- Beneficiaries of the IRA do not have to pay income tax after the IRA owner's death as long as the account is older than five years.

How to Implement Each IRA Plan

So now you know the difference between both kinds of IRA. For the finer details, I am sure your financial advisor will fill in the blanks. For now, you need to know how to go about implementing each form of plan.

Traditional IRA Implementation:

The first step is to approach your chosen institution—be it a bank, finance company, mutual fund business, life insurance company, or stockbroker. Speak to them about opening a traditional IRA for you.

The next step is to choose the type of investments that will fund the IRA—annuities, mutual fund, and CDs for example. From there, you only have to make contributions up to the due date of your federal income tax return for that particular year. This does not include extensions!

Keep in mind that states vary in their protection of IRAs from creditors and in their treatment of taxes. Make sure you know exactly how yours will be treated.

Roth IRA Implementation:

Like you did with your traditional IRA, for your Roth account, you will need to approach a bank, stockbroker, financial institution, life insurance company, or mutual stock company and ask them if they will give you a Roth IRA.

At that point, you will need to choose your types of investment to fund your IRA. These will also include things like mutual funds, annuities, or CDs.

Then you will make contributions up to the due date of your federal income tax return for that year, not including extensions.

Again, keep in mind that different states protect their Roth IRAs differently from creditors. Tax treatment also varies between states, so make sure that you know what you are getting into.

The implementation of each of these IRAs should not be done on your own. I would suggest having at least one financial advisor to paddle you through the choppy waters of the process. Once your IRAs are up and running, you should check on them twice a year and review your reports thoroughly.

CHAPTER 5

Your Retirement Plan (Part 2)

"Retirement: It's nice to get out of the rat race, but you have to learn to get along with less cheese."

GENE PERRET

P hew! Things are getting a little more complicated now, but hang in there with me. We are still focusing on day 4, and so far you have learned about traditional IRAs and Roth IRAs.

The next part of this is to understand what a 401k is and why you need one. I will then compare it to a Roth IRA, and we can see how to implement them at the end.

The 401k Plan Defined

The good old 401k is that employer-sponsored retirement plan that is offered at many businesses around the U.S. It allows you, as the employee, to save and invest a small piece of your salary before taxes are taken out of it.

In a 401k, taxes are not paid until the money is withdrawn from the account. It is called a 401k because that is what the tax code was called. The bulk of employers used to offer pension funds, but these have become expensive, so they have been replaced.

If you are lucky, you may still be able to get a good pension fund. If not, a 401k may be your only choice at work now. With this account, you control how your money is eventually invested. There are plans that offer a spread of mutual funds that contain money market investments or stocks and bonds, or you can opt for target-date funds.

There are some restrictions involved when using 401ks, and in most cases, you will be unable to access the funds that the employer has put away for you. "Vesting" is what they call it when a company demands a certain amount of work time from you before you can access any of your 401k money.

This makes sure that the employee does not leave their job before the employer's contribution become vested, which is in the best interest of the business. There will be an administrator like an investment company or bank, and they will send you updates or performance reports on your 401k.

The Benefits and Trade Offs of 401k Plans

The new standard is to find a good job that offers a suitable 401k that will help you save and put money away for retirement. The plan has benefits and it has trade-offs, but if you understand how they work, you can learn to use them appropriately.

The Benefits of 401k Plans

- If your employer has the right vesting schedule, then you can receive "free" money if your contributions are matched by your employer.

- It is completely up to you to decide how much you want to save and how you are going to invest your 401k money. As long as it is within federal limits of course.

- Every time you contribute to your 401k, it is done with pretax dollars—meaning that you only pay taxes on those dollars after they have been drawn out.

- If you have a Roth 401k feature that contains after-tax dollars, there may be no tax benefit up front. However, just like a Roth IRA, you could withdraw TAX-FREE.

- Your 401k plan may have a loan option that could be made available to you for quick, accessible cash.

Unlike IRAs, if you leave employment, you could access your 401k money as early as age 55.

The Trade Offs:

- No 401k plans promise future benefits, which means that at any time your plan investments can perform badly, and you can lose everything—or a lot of money. This is not ideal, but, unfortunately, it does happen.

- The IRS limits the amount of money that you can contribute to your 401k, which means that in many cases, it is not enough for retirement on its own.

- You might have to work for your employer for six years to gain access to their matching contributions—unless you have a simple 401k, a safe harbor 401k, or a qualified automatic contribution arrangement.

Comparing Roth 401k and Roth IRA Plans

There are Roth 401ks and Roth IRAs, but how do they compare? In order to better understand how each of these plans function, see how they match up in this brief comparison.

Roth 401k Plan:

- The maximum contribution for a 401k is less than $17,500 or 100% of compensation.

- There is a catch-up contribution of $5,500 available if you are 50 or older.

- Any eligible employee can contribute to a 401k.

- A 401k does require distributions after the age of 70 and a half, though it has a potential employer matching contribution.

- There is unlimited creditor protection in bankruptcy, and you are able to take out loans against your 401k if your plan permits it.

- From the time you contribute to the plan, there is a five-year waiting period for qualified distributions.
- Distributions are available on termination of employment, at age 55, and during hardship, disability, or death.
- There are qualified tax-free distributions at 59 and a half and during disability or death, and there are pro-rata distributions of tax-free contributions and taxable earnings.
- Rollovers to a Roth IRA, Roth 401k, Roth 403b, or from a Roth 401k or Roth 403b. As for investment choices, these are limited to investments offered by the employer.

Roth IRA:

- The maximum contribution for a Roth IRA is $5,500.00 or up to 100% of earned income, whichever is less.
- There is a catch-up contribution available if you are 50 or older of $1,000.00.
- A Roth IRA does not require any distributions, but it does not have any matching contributions from anyone.
- There could be a five-year waiting period from the time you contribute to any Roth IRA.
- Distributions are always available at any time. Qualified tax-free distributions are available at 59 and a half, during disability or death, or as a first-time homebuyer. Tax-free contributions are distributed first, then taxable earnings.
- Rollovers to and from a Roth IRA, from a Roth 401k or Roth 403b, and from a traditional IRA, 401k, 403b, or 457b. There are virtually unlimited investment choices here.

The Annuities Plan Defined

An annuity is simply an insurance contract between you and the insurance company.

A retirement annuity is another kind of investment fund that is very similar to an IRA. The main difference is that you have to buy an annuity contract, and this is contingent on a number of conditions.

The individual retirement annuity must be in the owner's name, and only the owner and their named beneficiaries will be able to get any kind of benefit from the contract. I would suggest caution when working with annuities as they are all different.

Sometimes there can be high fees, and they will not pay off like other investments do. However, there is always that "peace of mind" element that people want—and when you could outlive your income, annuities could bridge the gap.

Once you have purchased your annuity, it will pay out income to you for a set amount of time. Steady, predictable income streams are what annuities bring to the table.

First you invest in the annuity, then it will pay a certain amount out to you based on a series of predetermined dates. It can be monthly, quarterly, annually—or a whole lump sum payment. It is your choice entirely.

These payments can be received for the rest of your life or for a set number of years. It can be used to bridge a gap in income if you ever run out of your other funds. There are four types of annuity: fixed, variable, equity indexed, and immediate annuity.

The Benefits and Trade Offs of Annuities Plans

When thinking about buying an annuity, you should consider the benefits and the trade-offs that you get when working with this type of investment.

The Benefits of Annuities:

- The interest that is generated by your annuity accrues tax deferred until you withdraw the money.
- You are able to get payments from your annuity for the rest of your life, regardless of how long you may live.

- Normally, there are no contribution limits; it can be as high or as low as you want. There are many different forms of annuity to choose from, so finding a good one that suits your needs is important.

- You will pay taxes on the earnings portion of your annuity payments. Then, at death, the proceeds from your annuity will bypass probate to your named beneficiary.

The Trade Offs:

- There can be very high fees associated with variable annuities, and these expenses can cost you a lot of money in the long run. There may also be surrender changes involved.

- Contributions to your annuity are, of course, not tax deductible. There could be penalties for early withdrawals if you are younger than 59½.

- Then, once you select a specific distribution plan, annuitize the annuity, and begin getting payments, your election is irrevocable.

When you receive a pay-out of your annuity, on a monthly basis for example, you are subject to the same tax rules as normal. With variable annuities, your investment returns and the main value of the available sub-account portfolios will fluctuate or change based on the underlying performance of your assets.

This happens so that when your investor's units are redeemed, they can be worth more or less than their original value. However, from a fixed or immediate annuity, you will simply get a fixed dollar amount.

How to Implement Each Retirement Plan

Implementing either an employer sponsored plan or on your own is a choice that you have to make together as a couple. These are just vehicles for retirement, but the choices that you make now will impact you for your entire period of retirement.

With your 401k, contact your Human Resources (HR) department and ask for a retirement benefits package. The package should explain when employees become eligible, matching contribution, if any, and your investment options.

With your personal plans, you can approach the usual financial institutions—banks, insurance companies, investment companies; they will all have something to offer you. Do not be afraid to shop around if you cannot find what you want.

Keep in mind that you will need a diversified portfolio. The earlier you start to invest, the more you will be able to contribute over the course of your working life.

When you start early, your investments have a longer period of time to grow and compound, leaving you with more money and more choices when you reach retirement age.

As a rule of thumb, you should assess your risk tolerance once a year. Once you have done that, determine your investing time frame to see how much you will be able to invest. Then sit down and calculate exactly how much money you must invest to be where you need to be in old age.

Choose your investments according to your lifestyle, your risk tolerance, and how much time you have to put money away. If all of this is still too confusing, seek help. This is not the kind of area that does well with guesses.

Couples that guess their way to retirement planning end up getting way less than they thought—or worse. You must purposefully and consciously understand each and every investment vehicle and how it is benefitting you in your retirement years.

Then you need to keep up to date with them, monitor them, and ask questions if you see that something is not right. Remember: this is your money. Ultimately, you are responsible with your retirement.

CHAPTER 6

Investments, Risk, and Asset Allocation

"It's not whether you're right or wrong that's important, but how much money you make when you're right and how much you lose when you're wrong."

GEORGE SOROS

It is day 5, which means that we are diving in deeper to understand different types of investments and their associated risks in your retirement years. In this section, I will take you through what stocks, bonds, cash, and mutual funds are, as well as what their roles are in your portfolio.

Today you will decide if any of these additional investment vehicles are worth your time and consideration. Like the previous section on retirement planning, this one is split into two chapters. Let's begin with stocks.

The Ins and Outs of Stock

Stocks are popular because historically—on the financial scale—they provide higher long-term return than bonds and cash equivalents. Unfortunately, this also makes them more risky. When you buy a company's stock, you are buying a share of ownership in that company.

The percentage of shares that you own represents the share of risk that you have taken and the profits generated by the company. If your chosen company does well, your share of the profit will be proportionate to the amount of shares that you own in the company.

The same can be said if the company does badly; your losses will be equal to the shares you own. When you buy stock, you make money in one of two ways. Either you receive dividends as a stockholder, which is additional income for you, or you can sell your stock if the company does well and the value of the stock rises. This is known as a capital appreciation or capital gain.

There are loads of different types of stock and many different ways to diversify the stock that you hold. Growth stocks are stocks that earn at a faster rate than other stocks in their industry. Income stocks offer higher dividend yields than market averages. Value stocks sell at a low price relative to the company's book value or earnings.

You could end up losing part or all of your money. Do not count on stock as a short-term investment. Some people love playing with stock, but you have to decide whether you can afford to play around with your money.

Working With Bonds and Retirement

A bond is like an IOU. They are sometimes called fixed-income securities and are loans made to a corporation or governmental body.

The borrower (or bond issuer) promises to pay the lender (you) regular interest payments until a certain date. When this date arrives, the bond has "matured." Then the full amount of the loan must be repaid.

Bonds pay a stated interest rate, called a coupon. Most of these bonds pay interest on a fixed schedule—quarterly or semi-annually. Some do pay interest at maturity though. There are two main ways that you can profit from bonds.

The first is from the interest that the bond pays you. The second is to sell the bond for more than you paid for it. With any security, prices move up and down according to demand. A bond sold before its maturity date may be worth more or less than its original value.

There are some good reasons to choose bonds—their steady and predictable income streams via interest for example. When you are retired, it helps to have another income source that can supplement your existing funds and policies.

Bonds are not risk-free, however; many bond issuers can default on payment or fail to repay their principal. It depends on the company! They are considered safer than stocks, but they are still high-risk investments.

If a company declares bankruptcy, the bondholders can claim on the company's assets and cash flows. Depending on the type of bonds, the priority will be based on whether the bond is a secured or unsecured bond. A secured bond is when the company pledges specific collateral such as property, equipment, or other assets that the company owns. Therefore, if the company defaults, holders of secured bonds will have a legal right to foreclose on the collateral asset to satisfy their claims.

If the bonds are not considered a secured bond, they are unsecured and may be called debentures. Debentures have a general claim on the company's assets and cash flows. They may be classified as either senior or junior debentures. If the company defaults, senior debentures holders will have a higher priority claim over junior debentures.

Keep in mind that bondholders are not the only company's creditors. They may also owe money to the IRS, employee wages, banks, customers, suppliers, etc. In case of a company's default, they may have higher claims than certain bondholders.

How Does Cash Work?

Cash and cash alternatives are the next type of retirement investment that you could go for. Some examples of cash investments are: checking account, savings account, money markets, very short-term CDs (certificate of deposit), treasury bills, etc. They typically provide the lowest rate of return and the lowest potential for principal risk. However, you take on the inflation risk that the return you get may not keep up with the cost of living. For an example, if you had a money market account that pays 1% and the costs of goods and services are going up an average of 3% annually, you are not keeping up with the current purchasing power as you did year ago.

The ultimate advantage of these investments is that it can be converted into cash more quickly. When you focus on playing it safe with your money, you may entirely limit your return on investment—especially over long periods of time. That means that you will only earn small amounts on your investment over many years.

These cash alternatives can be useful—they provide relative stability—as far as getting your money back is concerned.

The risk is lower but so is your income. Sometimes not diversifying enough can result in slow growth and tragically small gains over many years. They can, however, provide an income for you on cash that would otherwise be idle.

Access to readily available cash should help see you through any financial emergencies, so it makes sense to have between 6–12 months of your expenses in cash investments. As a side note, beyond 6 to 12 months of your expenses, any money that you are planning on spending within the next 12 months also should be in a cash vehicle. For an example, if you are putting aside money for the down payment for a new house, car, vacation, or other big purchases, you simply do not want to take unnecessary risk by investing in stocks or bonds and potentially losing money right before you make the withdrawal to make the purchase.

Cash Alternatives and Retirement

As an asset class, this low-risk type of investment is something you should consider for low returns at a steady pace. The best investors in the world have all three: stocks, bonds, and cash alternatives.

The liquidity of the cash alternatives acts as something of a safety net when they are also investing in stocks and bonds. Let's take a look at different types of cash alternatives in more detail.

- *Money market funds*: This is part of the conservative cash alternative investment strategy. This type of fund tries to preserve the value of your investment at $1 per share, although—like all investments—this is not guaranteed. There are interest rate risks and inflation risks to consider.

- *Stable value funds*: A stable value fund is often found in a 401k. They are collective trust funds or accounts created specifically for your employer's retirement plan offering. These provide a greater return on investment over time than money market funds. There is low volatility here, which is why they are so stable.

It can be fairly confusing trying to decide how to diversify your retirement portfolio because within every type of asset class, there are many subtypes with their own unique sets of rules and risks.

Before investing in alternative assets, make sure that you have a thorough understanding of exactly what they are and how they might perform or tank. Cash alternatives can be a very important part of your portfolio—price stability and liquidity potential is there even though there are lower rates of return.

These days you can find very specialized cash alternatives, with products differing from one to the other. I would also advise you to take a long look at the fees and expenses structure of your cash investment as you can lose money in the wrong product.

Accumulating Mutual Funds

So how do you go about investing in stocks, bonds, and cash alternatives when either you do not have the time to do your own research or do not want to hand pick your own? You can invest in all three of these types of investments through mutual funds. Mutual funds pool your money with money from other investors. There is a professional fund manager, and they will select which securities to buy based on a presented investment strategy.

These mutual funds offer many benefits, but there are two that stand out. Because mutual funds own hundreds of securities, there is greater diversification than you would have buying individual securities on your own.

Plus, you have a fund manager's expertise at your service, and you pay for it while they manage your mutual funds. Professional money management, diversification, and liquidity are all high points for mutual funds.

The fund can invest in one of three of the asset classes or combine them for greater reach. A well-balanced fund usually contains stocks, bonds, and cash. The fund manager will buy and sell these securities while trying to beat the benchmark index.

A passive fund will match the return on a specific index by holding the securities included in that index. Some of the funds attempt to tailor the asset allocation to your risk tolerance and how soon you expect to use your invested money.

These funds are called target-date funds—they focus on adjusting your asset allocation based on your given date—shifting investments over time to increase capital preservation as your date approaches. That means higher risk in the beginning and lower risk at the end.

These target-date funds are available in series. When the investor expects to withdraw and use their money is the date that is assigned to the fund. If you retire in 2030, you will set up your fund to start releasing money at the right times.

For the rest of the time, you will be earning and investing. While nothing is 100% assured in finance, mutual funds are safer from losing all of your money at once because if the mutual funds holds 100 stocks in the portfolio, all of those 100 companies have to belly up in one single day in order to lose all of it. However, if you only had one single stock and that company went bankrupt, you could lose it all.

Here is the list of bankrupt companies you may recognize, to name a few: Lehman Brothers, WorldCom, Enron, Washington Mutual, Delta, Chrysler, GM.

Exchange Traded Funds Defined

An exchange traded fund is a security that tracks an index, commodity, or group of assets like an index fund but trades like stock does on the stock exchange. ETFs go through price fluctuations repeatedly throughout the day as they are bought and sold.

Think of ETFs as being like a mutual fund but trading like a stock. ETFs have been around since 1993, and they are very popular today.

While a mutual fund is an investment—brimming with different shares, stocks, bonds, and cash alternatives—and is managed by a Fund manager, it differs from an ETF. The prices of mutual funds do not vary during the day because prices are set at the end of the day.

With exchange traded funds, there are some similarities to mutual funds, namely it is also a pool of investments. But unlike mutual funds, ETFs typically have much lower expenses than mutual funds.

ETFs do not trade at the end of the day like mutual funds do. They are directly determined by investor demand at any given time, live throughout the day. These ETFs are bought and sold like stocks and bonds.

There is a bid price from buyers and an asking price from sellers. ETFs are also more tax effective than mutual funds. They can decrease or avoid capital gain distributions because they are traded just like stocks are.

CHAPTER 7

Investments, Risk, and Asset Allocation (Part 2)

"When I was young I thought that money was the most important thing in life; now that I am old I know that it is."

OSCAR WILDE

It is the second part of day 5, which means that by now you are knee-deep in choosing the investments that you want to make for your retirement portfolio.

Without mutual fund diversification, you will have to manually decide which investments to make to maintain balanced asset allocation and diversity. In this section, you will find out more about the many investments that you can make.

The Different Types of Annuities

We are going to discuss more in detail on different types of annuities. Even the greatest IRAs and employer-sponsored plans can sometimes not be enough when you want to retire with a suitable income in old age. To answer the question what happens if I want to save more, annuities are generally the answer.

There are several different types of annuities that you could invest in. These are:

- *Immediate annuities*: An immediate annuity starts paying out shortly after the premium is paid. You can buy one with a single premium, and the contract is usually irrevocable once you have signed it.

  Assets do not accumulate as tax-deferred but are distributed using a formula—like "for life" or for fixed periods and fixed amounts. There are two types of Immediate Annuities. They are either Fixed or Variable Immediate Annuity. With a fixed immediate annuity, you lock in a fixed income stream for your entire life or a specific number of years, if you choose. With a variable immediate annuity, you could potentially keep up with the inflation or purchasing power. However, your monthly income could be higher or lower due to actual investment results of mutual fund-like portfolios.

- *Why you want this*: For either fixed or variable income for the rest of your life

- *Why you do not want this*: Loss of purchasing power with a fixed annuity or potentially receive less monthly income form investment loss with a variable annuity. You also lose control of the premium that you paid to purchase this immediate annuity.

- *Fixed annuities*: Minimum guaranteed interest is paid with fixed annuities; there is a minimum death benefit but no possibility of losing your principal due to fluctuation in investment values. There are no multiple investment options. This option can help you sleep at night knowing that the account value will go up steadily over time. However, the interest you earn may not keep up with inflation. Later, you could convert it into an immediate annuity by term, known as annuitization.

- *Why you want this*: Guaranteed rates of interest
- *Why you do not want this:* Low interest rate and may not keep up with inflation; heavy surrender charges if you cancel the contract early

- *Variable annuities*: There are multiple investment options. There is no minimum guaranteed interest paid with variable annuities, but there is a death benefit. There is also a chance of losing your principal due to fluctuations in investment values.

- *Why you want this*: Gives you the opportunity to pump up your savings by giving you a chance for long-term capital growth. This gives you the potential to outpace inflation.

- *Why you do not want this*: Simply, you are taking investment risk. That means that you could lose money if your chosen investments perform poorly. Capital gains inside variable annuities are treated as an Ordinary Income Tax when you withdrawal rather than Long-Term Capital Gains Tax. Therefore, potentially, you could face a higher tax rate.

- *Equity-Indexed annuities*: This provides a guaranteed interest with some upside. For an example, the contract may state that this equity-indexed annuity pays the higher of a minimum return of 2% or tied to the performance of the Standard & Poor's 500 index up to 6%. What that really means is that your annual interest could be between 2% and 6% annually, but it cannot be lower than 2% or higher than 6%.

  - *Why you want this*: It gives you the opportunity to participate in the upside when the stock market is climbing and also protects against the downside since it has a minimum interest even if the stock market is a negative for the year.

  - *Why you do not want this*: Some are very complex, and it can be hard to calculate your return on investments. You may not get the full upside potential, unlike a variable annuity. During a good year, the S&P 500 might be up 20%. However, you may still only receive 6% or what they call "annual cap."

Working With Structured Notes

Once you have discussed the various types of annuities, you will need to lean in close and investigate the other kinds of investment alternatives that exist. These extras can make up an important part of your retirement portfolio, so do not leave them out.

A structured note is a debt obligation that contains a derivative component with characteristics that adjust the securities risk and return profile. In plain English, it is a type of hybrid security that allows for additions of other reference assets or benchmarks.

A decent example is a 10-year bond tied or linked together with an option contract. The way the security is arranged is in this structured note form. This type of investment offers investors potential returns that are higher than interest rates on traditional deposits.

Capital appreciation depends on the performance of the underlying reference assets—which is a greater risk than simply making a traditional deposit. In what kind of circumstances would you choose to invest in structured notes? Avoid them if you...

- Want higher returns than most traditional products but you are not prepared for variable returns that could lose your entire investment amount.

- Do not understand how payouts work in a structured note; do not invest in one, because they are extremely varied.

- Do not understand the risk potential; if not, then do not invest in this security. Plus, these investments usually have a maturity date, so if you need access to your cash at all times, this may not be the right portfolio investment for you.

Structured notes pay interest or returns at regular intervals. This is according to the formula or fixed coupon structure outlined in the contract. You will get your money at maturity plus interest if all goes well.

The best advice I can give you here is to properly explore this option with your financial advisor. See how it fits with your portfolio; otherwise, move onto something else.

Non-Traded REIT and BDC Alternative Investments

The next two kinds of alternative investment are focused on diversifying your portfolio with non-traded real estate investment trusts and non-traded business development companies.

Non-traded investments are not traded on the securities exchange. Therefore, you cannot turn it into cash, or it remains illiquid for a certain period of time. They operate similar to mutual funds. However, non-traded REIT or BDC are non-correlated asset classes; they could help you lower or limit the volatility of your portfolio.

The first of them is Non-traded REIT, or Real Estate Investment Trusts. This is a form of real estate investment that is designed to generate steady income and is not tied directly to the stock market.

The key benefit with any Non-traded REIT is that they are not yet publically traded, but you still get the advantages of having a REIT. It usually provides stable cash flow without the volatility that is present in public markets.

Non-traded REITs also get the same great tax benefits by meeting certain requirements for taxable income distribution to shareholders.

- *Why you want this*: Generate income from big commercial buildings, industrial warehouses, hotels, etc. You probably will not be able to purchase them on your own. Many times, these purchases require you to invest millions of dollars out of pocket.
- *Why you do not want this*: Lack of liquidity. If you need the funds to be available sooner than 7–10 years, do not invest in them.

A Non-traded Business Development Company (BDC) is a company that invests in the debt or equity of private companies and must be regulated by certain provisions under the Investment Company Act of 1940.

Investment options for Non-traded BDCs include equity and debt. They are supposed to generate income and, to a certain extent, capital appreciation. When a BDC invests in the equity of a private company, it is almost the same as investing in stock. However, that private equity (stock) is not publicly traded on the market.

Debt, on the other hand, is similar to bonds in a public company. The BDC is the lender to the company and provides contractual returns and repayment priorities. For public companies, there are stocks and bonds; for private companies, there is debt and equity.

Take into account the limited liquidity and the fact that at any time the plan can be cancelled, changed, or suspended, which means that you may lose money.

- *Why you want this*: Similar to non-traded REIT, it could create an investment portfolio that generates superior risk-adjusted returns. When you diversify your investments over non-correlated asset classes, it also helps you lower or limit the volatility of your portfolio.
- *Why you do not want this*: Lack of liquidity. If you need the funds to be available sooner than 7–10 years, do not invest in them.

What Is Your Risk Tolerance?

Investing is a different experience for everyone. Based on your own set of predetermined goals and restrictions, the type of retirement investment portfolio that you manage is entirely up to you. The first step to determining what that will be is to understand risk.

It is impossible for you as an investor to avoid risk altogether, so you will need to manage it according to what you are willing to do, or not willing to do. There are three main types of investor: aggressive, moderate, and conservative.

People with a high degree of risk tolerance are aggressive, and it scales down from there. You are considered a conservative investor if you will only tolerate low risk investments. There is a direct relationship that exists between risk and return: the lower the risk, the lower the return—the higher the risk, the higher the return.

To manage risk, answer these important tolerance questions:

- When do you plan to get principle withdrawals from your portfolio?
- How old are you?
- How long do you want your long-term investments to be?
- If you owned investments that fell 20% in a short period, what would you do?
- Rate how much you agree: You prefer investments with little or no fluctuation in value and will accept lower returns associated with those investments.
- During times of market decline, you tend to sell some riskier assets and put the money in safer places. Rate on a scale of strongly agree to strongly disagree.
- When it comes to stocks, bonds, and mutual funds, what is your experience level?
- How do rising and falling market fluctuations affect you emotionally?
- Which investment would you feel most comfortable owning: CDs, government bonds, stocks of established companies, or stocks of new companies?
- How optimistic are you about long-term economic prospects?
- What is your ideal portfolio value in 10 years' time?
- What is your current income requirement for your portfolio? (in percentages)

If you can answer these questions, you will get a better idea of what your personal risk tolerance is as a couple. Showing these answers to your financial advisor will give them a great idea of what kind of investment portfolio you are looking for.

Balancing Asset Allocation

All portfolios should contain a liberal mix of investments that you have chosen to personally balance out your risk so that you can endure any losses that may happen over time. Asset allocation is one of the first steps that you take when you want to create a diverse portfolio.

You need to decide how your investment dollars should be allocated among your broad investment classes, cash alternatives, stocks, and bonds—this is known as asset allocation. There are different rates of return for each of the different classes and varying levels of price fluctuation.

Your investments will often respond to the same news, which means that as your stocks plummet, your bonds may rapidly rise; it all depends on the source that changes the market. When you diversify your investments over non-correlated asset classes, it also helps you lower or limit the volatility of your portfolio.

The way in which you choose to diversify will impact your eventual gains. That said, there is no guarantee that your widely diverse investment portfolio will make a profit. There is always a possibility of loss in the investment arena, and it is important that you know that.

So how do you choose the right mix? There are lots of great tools and asset allocation samples that you can look over, but streamlining these to your own needs is critical. There will always be objective variables and subjective variables to take into account (age and risk tolerance for example).

At the end of the day, you need to choose a mix of investments that have the potential to provide you with the kind of return that you want at the level of risk that you are most comfortable with.

This is why many people choose to hire a financial advisor; they can help you gain insight into what your risk tolerance may be, then they can customize a portfolio for you that is in line with your financial situation.

Learning to Monitor Your Retirement Portfolio

As a couple, your retirement portfolio investments are supposed to be a carefully planned and prepared approach to managing and accumulating money over time. This is so that you can benefit from the longest possible investment period and compound interest.

It is important to do this so that you are able to stay ahead of inflation, which reduces the purchasing power of your dollar with every passing year. At 3% annual inflation, something that costs $100.00 will cost $180.00 in some 20 years.

You need to see annual growth in your retirement portfolio so that your investments stay on track throughout your working life. That means monitoring your retirement portfolio carefully via your financial advisor or the company that you are dealing with.

That way, if you invest $5,000.00 right now and then every year after that, in 30 years—with good management—you will have invested $150,000.00. If your funds grow at 6% annually, you can look forward to having almost $420,000 in that account. Not bad!

The two keys to adequately monitoring your portfolio are finding the right financial advisor (who will keep you updated with reports) and making sure that you hold yourself accountable and keep your eyes on your portfolio.

Anything can happen with financial markets and investing. The whole point of a great retirement portfolio is for it to be as diverse as possible.

When you are always fully aware of what your investments are doing—and your financial advisor is constantly working for your success—then you have a good thing. I suggest reviewing your portfolio performance at least once a quarter to stay in touch with changes or to make decisions on your investments.

CHAPTER 8

Asset Protection

"Life is constantly providing us with new funds, new resources, even when we are reduced to immobility. In life's ledger there is no such thing as frozen assets."

HENRY MILLER

Day 6 has arrived, which means that you are really starting to gain a clear picture of what your retirement portfolio should look like. At this stage, you need to consider how insurance will impact your life and where you need to cover yourself for your future.

In this section, I will go over the various types of insurance that you need in your life and how each of them can give you peace of mind, especially as you approach retirement age one day.

Learning About Auto Insurance

At this point in your life, you will need auto or car insurance, and it is something to consider for old age as well. Unlike other forms of insurance, car insurance actually gets less expensive the older that you get.

That means that when you approach retirement age, you should look into reapplying for insurance to take advantage of the many senior benefits available. Unless you have been marked as a high risk driver, you will almost surely qualify for reduced fees.

People of retirement age are some of the most experienced drivers on the road—they have been doing it for a very long time. They are also among the most mature on the road, which means they are not likely to ramp over pavements because they are upset that their boyfriend has broken up with them, again.

- Auto insurance companies will often offer bundle coverage, and they will sell you a car while at the same time insuring your vehicle.

- You can reduce your insurance rates if you buy a car specifically with a high safety rating. Seatbelts, airbags...run down the insurance checklist and get your rates reduced based on the required safety features.

- Get your car insured for theft so that you do not lose an asset at any time that you cannot recover. Anti-theft alarms and devices should be installed and used to reduce your potential for theft.

- If you structure your payments differently, you can often negotiate better rates with your insurance company. Paying once every three months or twice a year (every six months), will lower your monthly fees.

- Always maintain a good driving record to take advantage of the reduction in fees, and try to renew your insurance policy with the same company so that you can benefit from long-term customer discounts.

Maintaining a balanced portfolio means knowing what you pay for car insurance right now and making sure that you never have to pay more for something that should be relatively inexpensive by following the rules.

There are four main types of auto insurance, namely liability, uninsured/underinsured, collision and comprehensive, and personal injury. Having complete cover is important, so it is a goal that you need for yourself.

Insight on Home Insurance

To protect your properties throughout your life and towards retirement age, you need to focus on the right kind of home insurance.

Your home is often the largest asset you will own in your lifetime, and it is critical that you protect and insure this asset so you do not lose all of your equity one day. Most companies demand that you take out replacement-value house insurance.

When theft, fire, and storm damage happens, you will need an insurer to cover it. They do not typically insure you for natural disasters, but if you stay in a high risk area, you should consider taking out additional coverage.

The type of coverage you get is dictated by the agreement that you make with your chosen home insurance company. Typically, it consists of the following:

- The dwelling coverage will make sure that if your home is damaged structurally, it will be fixed. This includes damage to fixtures, plumbing, electrical wiring, and heating and cooling systems throughout the house.
- Other structures like tool sheds, fences, garages, guest cottages, and any other structure that is not attached to your house
- Personal property, which will reimburse you for the value of your possessions—including furniture, electronics, appliances, clothing, and even off-site insurance
- Personal liability covers you for financial loss if you are sued or found legally responsible for damages to other property or people.
- Loss of use will pay for some of your additional living expenses while your house is being repaired.
- Medical payments; if anyone is ever hurt on your property this insurance coverage will take care of the expenses.

As life continues, these little "upsets" can cause an average American family to fall into bankruptcy if they are not protected. That is why insurance is so important. Not only do you need to protect your key property assets, you also need to protect your financial interest in your belongings, home, and family health and wellness.

Health Insurance

You and your spouse will need to settle on comprehensive health insurance as soon as you can. There are many different types to choose from, and a lot of companies that will try to tell you that their cover is the best.

The challenge is to sit down and wade through all of your choices, so that you can really find the cover that suits your lifestyle and covers your health needs. Many people have existing health concerns such as diabetes, or asthma etc.

Many health insurance companies use profiling for coverage, but you need to look beyond that – and take your needs, income, and risk profile into account. The last thing you want is to get into a position where you really need the coverage, but you do not have it.

- HMO's are the health maintenance organizations that will offer you a set of basic plans to choose from. They are commonly tiered from bronze to platinum*.
- POS plans or point of service plans have a wider range of choice than your standard HMO plans. You can choose to see doctors or visit hospitals outside of your network, and your monthly payments will be higher because of that.
- Preferred provider organizations are a newish kind of health plan that focus on networks of doctors, medical centers and hospitals that are part of a group, and as such – they agree to charge less for group members.
- An HDHP or high-deductible health plan does (as the name

---

* 4 Types of Health Plans: How They Compare, http://www.webmd.com/health-insurance/insurance-basics/types-of-health-insurance-plans

suggests) have a higher deductible than other plans, but the premiums are lower. Deductibles are the amounts that you will pay before your health plan pays for anything. You will pay lower rates each month, but if you ever claim – costs will be higher, and you may have to fork over your own cash before approval.

The best way to get a good health insurance coverage is to get them through your Employer's group benefit. IF your employer does not provide one, private health insurance may be ideal for you and your spouse as a young couple, depending on your current health status. Realistically, medical costs are so astronomical this is not an area you can cut back on.

If your health falls apart, so does everything else and more than one couple has regretted not taking out comprehensive, or at least partially comprehensive coverage for their 'hard working' years. Accidents, disease and minor procedures do happen, and they can bankrupt you quicker than anything else in your life.

Sit with your spouse and discuss your options. Assess your current health status, and make a list of the features that you need in your coverage. Is chronic disease medication covered? Is there an area of medicine that you must include in your coverage, due to your patient history? Health insurance can be expensive, but rather pay too much than too little as a rule.

Choosing the Right Life Insurance

Once you have decided on the right car and home insurance, you will need to sit down and discuss life insurance, which is slightly more complicated. Life insurance is a contract between you and your insurer.

In your stated terms, your insurer agrees to pay a certain sum to the person of your choice upon your death in exchange for premium payments. The right kind of life insurance should give you peace of mind that your family will be financially solvent if you pass away.

Life insurance has many purposes, namely to replace your income for your family if you die. It is also a way for your family to pay off any debt that you may have on passing. How much you take out depends on several factors: marital status, family size, career, and the goals that you have in life.

There are lots of ways to determine how much coverage to get. Grab a pen and write down what your immediate financial expenses would be for your family after death. Outline how much of your current salary is devoted to expenses and how long your dependents would need support. How much money do you want to leave to your family?

The final question, of course, is how much coverage can you realistically afford? Things like age, wellness, physical condition, and fitness level all matter. Once you know what you can afford, you will be asked to sign a life insurance contract.

There are two main kinds of life insurance contracts: term life and permanent (cash value) life. Term life is limited coverage for a specific amount of time; if you pass while covered, your family will get the policy amount. If you live past the term, the policy terminates itself.

Permanent insurance policies protect you for life. The premiums are greater during the early years of the policy to make sure that it can be covered when you eventually do pass away one day. There are four basic categories: whole life, universal life, variable life, and variable universal life. These are premium payment structures, so choose wisely.

Once you have named your primary beneficiary and paid your first installment, your policy comes into effect. As you sit together, discuss the various types of insurance and what kind of coverage you are looking for. Then compare it to what you can afford.

Having Appropriate Disability Insurance

Great, so you have found a decent life insurance policy, what next? No one likes to think about this next section, but it is a reality that must be considered. Disability insurance will pay you benefits if you become sick or injured and unable to earn a living.

This coverage replaces your income should you become unable to work for a period of time. Your chances of becoming disabled for a short period of time are greater than your chances of dying at a young age, which means that at some point, your family could face financial turmoil unless you prepare for it.

Your income is an asset of yours, and it needs to be protected to maintain your financial portfolio. If you could not work for six months or six years, how would you generate income? It is so easy to become disabled and duly overwhelmed with financial burden as a result.

Once you become disabled, you have to apply for your benefits, which can take some time. Individual disability insurance may make you wait 90–365 days for payment, while group insurance policies take only eight days to kick in.

You can buy disability coverage that lasts until retirement age. Most people will invest in a policy that will pay benefits up to the age of 65. There are also policies that will pay you partially and allow you to still earn an income if you are able.

As a couple, you need to determine how much disability coverage you need. This really depends on the answers to these three core questions:

- How much income will you need to replace if you become disabled?
- How much money can you afford to spend on premiums?
- How much insurance can you buy under your insurer's guidelines?

Check with your employer to see if you are covered for disability through a work-based policy. If you are, most likely your company is paying the premium as a group benefit. If they do pay for your premiums and you became disabled and collect the income, understand that you have to pay income tax on the collected amount. Therefore, you may want to consider purchasing supplemental insurance through work or on your own. If you pay the premiums out of pocket, your collected disability income becomes TAX-FREE. You will also need to anticipate the rise of your medical needs, which will have to be covered if you do become unable to work.

The maximum you can usually get is 66–70% of your existing income, which should be good enough to keep you going in the event of a serious accident. Having disability coverage will make sure that you do not lose everything you have worked for if something happens!

Long-term Care Insurance

Planning for long-term care is the final insurance concern that you and your spouse need to seriously consider. The truth is that some 70% of people will need long-term care at some point during their lifetime once they have reached the age of 65.

There are so many people living with Alzheimer's (14%) after the age of 71; that is why it makes sense to plan for your eventual care in a suitable facility or nursing home. Younger people may also have need for long-term care in the event of accident or illness.

Every year, long-term care costs a little more. It is incredibly expensive and something that you do not want to overlook now because it will impact you in your old age. The average cost to stay in a nursing home for one year is $74,820.00, and there are states where this amount is even higher.

Costs rise steadily by 3% a year or more. In some 20 years, you could be looking at $135,133.00 per year. It is easy, then, to understand that this is something you have to factor into your retirement planning now while you still have the time to afford it.

Too many senior citizens lose their entire life savings and retirement portfolio because of expensive nursing homes, leaving their families with little to no inheritance at all. With proper planning, you can ensure that you get premium, quality care in your old age.

There are three main levels of long-term care: skilled, intermediate, and custodial. Skilled care is round-the-clock care that is provided by a nurse or alternative medical professional. Intermediate care involves medical staff but is not full time, and custodial care involves a nurse assisting the senior in daily activities like bathing, eating, and dressing.

Long-term care is offered in nursing homes, assisted-living facilities, in your own home, and in adult day-care facilities. When you put your long-term care insurance plan together, make sure that it covers the various types of care that you may need.

CHAPTER 9

Adequate Estate Planning

"Preparation for old age should begin not later than one's teens. A life which is empty of purpose until 65 will not suddenly become filled on retirement."

ARTHUR E. MORGAN

It is day 7, and today I will be discussing the ins and outs of estate planning. Everyone needs to have an estate plan so that when they pass away, the estate is divided among the family and/or charities as the individual intended.

Typically, an estate plan consists of health care directives, durable power of attorney, and a will. However, a trust may be part of your estate planning strategy if you want to keep your private financial affairs from going through a probate.

Why You Need an Estate Plan

As I said, everyone needs to create an estate plan when they are sorting out their financial affairs. It is not something that just the wealthy do; in fact, smaller estates often require close attention, so it is important that these documents exist.

Your estate plan will allow you to make sure that your family or chosen loved ones will be provided for and not burdened by personal and financial concerns during the time of your passing. It makes your final wishes clear to your family and avoids any disputes over ownership that may arise when you are gone.

Estate planning is especially important if transfer taxes concern you or if you own property in more than one state. If you have kids—including grown kids with special needs—or you own a successful business, these are also concerns. You will also need one if your spouse is not comfortable handling the finances or if you want to make charitable donations when you pass away.

During your estate planning process, you will map out how your personal and financial matters should be handled during periods of incapacity or death. An estate plan should be implemented with the assistance of a decent estate planning attorney.

No one likes to plan for the day when they are going to die. But this is a reality that becomes more and more important, especially as your family grows. The last thing you want is to leave behind a spouse and kids with no way of supporting themselves.

Organizing Your Will

Your will is the most important document that you will outline in this section. It is known as your "last will and testament" and will include instructions about who should settle your estate, who will be the guardian of your children, and how your property will be distributed to your heirs.

A will is valid if you are of legal age and stable mind and when it is written, properly signed, properly witnessed. and properly executed. When you pass away, your will has to go through a process called probate, in which your executor files it with the probate court.

Your executor will also collect any monies that you are owed, will pay all of your outstanding bills, and will file any remaining tax returns. The distribution of property and the estate will then happen according to the terms you have outlined in your will.

To organize your will, take a moment and write down what your key assets are. Then list your debts and obligations. Name your executor and guardian for minor children, then comment on any charitable donations you want to make. It also helps if you stipulate where your important documents can be found.

Consider using witnesses that are complete strangers, as many states automatically disinherit witnesses. All of the formalities must be adhered to, or your estate could end up going elsewhere.

Make a point of reviewing your will periodically at certain events—like when you get divorced or add members to your family. Anything can happen at any time, and the people that take care of their wills always make the process so much easier for their families.

Keep in mind that if your estate is worth more than your exemption amount in the year that you die, you may end up having to pay estate taxes. You will have to work out how much they could be by assessing the value of gross estate, subtract debts, subtract expenses, subtract spouse money, subtract charity and exemption amount, and add in taxables.

The Other Estate Planning Documents

Sudden incapacity or death can seriously impact your family, cause financial devastation, and exhaust any and all savings that you may have had. A good estate planning strategy involves avoiding this outcome by making sure the other documents aside from your will are also included in your estate.

- *A living will* – This document details the types of medical treatment that you want or could need or do not want under special circumstances.
- *The DNR Order* – This Do Not Resuscitate order is a legal form that is signed by both you and your doctor, which gives hospital staff the permission to not resuscitate you, should that be your choice.
- *Medical durable power of attorney* – This allows one or more family members or trusted individuals to make medical decisions for you.

- *Living trust* – Your living trust is a successor trustee that will step into your shoes to manage property in the trust if something happens to you.

- *Joint ownership* – This document allows someone else to have the same access to your property as you do.

- *Financial durable power of attorney* – This allows you to name family members or other trusted individuals to make financial decisions or transact business on your behalf.

There is also the matter of lifetime gifting that you can discuss together now. Lifetime gifting is a personal estate planning strategy that has a lot of great benefits for your family. You can shift income-producing property to family members in lower tax brackets, or you can use portions of your estate tax exemptions now instead of at death.

Lifetime gifts include properties that you own, in the same state and in different states from where you live. You can get all kinds of great tax breaks and benefits if you decide to include this in your strategy, but you will need to discuss it more with a qualified financial professional or attorney.

The Dangers of Not Having an Estate Plan

You have probably heard the stories about that poor family who prematurely lost a key family member that did not have a will. What usually happens after that is awful for the family, and it can leave your entire life's work in ruins.

The question you need to ask yourself right now is—what happens if I die without a will? Unless you have put other estate planning strategies in place, your property will go to the person or people that your state's intestacy laws say it should go to.

These state intestacy laws specify how your property will be divided, and your actual wishes become completely irrelevant, even if you have unofficial documents that clearly outline what they are.

There are some very real dangers of not having an estate plan. Your loved ones may become overly burdened settling your estate without the help of advanced planning. They may be completely inadequately provided for, and your estate may not pass to your heirs according to your wishes.

If you fail to properly plan, even more of your estate may end up paying taxes and estate expenses than you ever may have realized. In a typical intestacy distribution that generally differs from state to state, they will give 1/3 to 1/2 of your estate to your spouse and the remainder to your children. This is regardless of who they are or what they meant to you.

The real danger here, as you can see, is that family—is not always that simple. Sometimes a child will not be included in the will for very good reasons, and the same goes for the spouse. If you do not take the time to fully document, in an official capacity, what happens to your investments and properties after death, it will cause dissention in your family.

This could lead to even more financial difficulty and the eventual dissolution of your entire estate, including all properties or interests, sold for cash that can be divided up between your family members. As you know, this is not always the best move to make. It can only be prevented if you make provision for it in your official will.

Saved! Your 529 Plan Explained

A large part of estate planning involves making provision for your kids to go to college one day. You may have a budding little Einstein in your pram right now, but they will amount to nothing if they cannot get into a good college one day.

College is enormously expensive, which means that you need to start planning and saving for it right away. Systematic college savings are best expressed with a 529 plan. It allows you to save for college without bankrupting you financially.

A 529 is a savings vehicle that is governed by the federal government but is offered by individual states. There are two main types of 529 plan: the college savings plan and the prepaid tuition plan.

- The college savings plan is an individual investment account that you will contribute to every month. You money is allocated to your choice of one of the plan's pre-established investment portfolios. Returns are not guaranteed, but you can use your savings at any accredited college.

All states offer a 529 savings plan for college. They are individual accounts, and you can make the decision to join any state's plan.

The prepaid tuition plan allows you to prepay your child's college tuition at today's prices. Whatever contribution you make right now is generally guaranteed to cover a certain percentage of college tuition when your kid is grown up. Your own state plan must be used, and your child is limited to the colleges there.

Unlike the college savings plan, this prepaid plan is generally for public, in-state colleges. It depends on what you want for your kids. If you plan on sending them to an Ivy League school, then the first type of 529 plan will work, especially if you live in another state.

If you just want to make sure they attend a good college, then a prepaid plan may work best for your financial needs and future goals. Discuss this together and decide. You should also take into account the amount of kids you plan on having, or already have.

Benefits of a 529 Plan

There is one clear benefit with a good 529 plan, and that is that your contributions grow tax deferred, and your earnings are completely tax free at the federal level when they are withdrawn to pay for your child's educational expenses.

Withdrawals that are not used for qualified expenses are still subject to the normal federal and state income tax, as well as a 10% penalty tax.

As an investor, you need to consider the risks, charges, expenses, and objectives that are involved in your potential 529 plan. Also take some time to find out if your state offers great state income tax benefits on your chosen 529.

Typically, the average American family struggles to afford college, and the only alternative ways to get funding is to apply for financial aid and for your child to work their way through the endless fees and expenses.

The benefits of a well-planned 529 are straightforward; your child will get to go to college without having to worry about where the money will come from to pay for it. They will be able to focus on their studies and live a better quality of life (job pays for living expenses not tuition), and they are free to enjoy the important college experience.

529 plans also offer another hidden benefit—that of estate planning advantages with accelerated gifting. Grandparents, for example, can contribute to their grandchildren's education while sizing down their own estate.

A lump-sum gift to a 529 plan of between $70,000.00 and $140,000.00 for married couples can be made, and you can still avoid the gift tax if it is treated as having been made in equal installments over a five-year period.

In this way, a 529 can help you put money away for your kids' college funds. Always check on your state's tax benefits and how they want you to invest in your 529 plan. It helps to run your strategy past a financial advisor in case you miss any minor details that matter.

The last thing you want is to realize that you have done something wrong 20 years later that affects the future of your kids' education.

It is far better to plan and take out a 529 and then review your investment there every year to stay on track.

Without a Will...

If you do not have a will, you can still take some basic steps you can do today that will cost you nothing to implement. That is naming beneficiaries in all of your financial accounts with either TOD (Transfer on Death) or POD (Payable on Death) in order to bypass probate.

TOD is used when you are naming a beneficiary on a brokerage or investment account. POD is used when naming a beneficiary on a bank account. You simply need to contact your bank and investment account providers and name the beneficiary.

Also, you can name a beneficiary on any retirement accounts, such as 401k, 403b, IRA, pension, etc. It will not be retitled with TOD or POD. However, once they have the beneficiary form on file, your financial institution will directly pay your beneficiary upon death.

CHAPTER 10

Social Security Strategy for Married Couples

"The rate of return on Social Security for people nearing retirement is about 1.5 percent. By the time young children like mine are ready to retire, that rate of return will be a negative percentage."

PAUL RYAN

You have arrived on day 8 of your retirement blueprint, and today let's focus on your Social Security strategy, specifically for married couples. Deciding when to begin receiving your Social Security benefits is key to a good retirement portfolio.

People that take their Social Security too early may miss out on important benefits that could make a real impact on your quality of life.

An Introduction to Social Security Strategy

Your choices with Social Security are fairly straightforward—take it early and receive less, or take it later and get more. There is no right answer if you really want to know; it all depends on your circumstances when you get there.

There are dozens of variables to take into account. For example, you may have fallen ill and exhausted your retirement portfolio. Then your only option is to take Social Security early so that you can cover your daily living expenses.

If, however, you plan well and have other sources of income—or you want to continue working through your old age—you may decide that waiting to collect Social Security benefits makes a lot more sense to you financially.

Take this time to learn about Social Security, and then make an informed, educated decision about when you are going to begin receiving your benefits. Consider these:

- What is the exact amount that you will receive from Social Security? Check on your earnings history, and if you can receive benefits earlier, later, or at full retirement age.

- How long do you plan your retirement to last? Life expectancy and several other factors can go into making this decision.

- How does this Social Security amount affect your overall retirement income plan? Take a look at your projected expenses again and where your income will be coming from other investment vehicles and streams.

- How will it affect your spouse? Retirement and survivor benefits need to be maximized if you are part of a married couple.

- Social Security can be taxed if you are getting income from other streams, so take this into account when working with the numbers.

Strategic Age and Benefit Planning

Social Security is actually a major source of retirement income for most people that end up retiring. The moment you begin taking your Social Security dictates how large your benefit will be. This is the most important factor when planning your strategic benefit.

Your particular benefit is based on the number of years that you have worked and the total amount of money that you have earned. When you become eligible for retirement benefits at the age of 62, the SSA, or Social Security Administration, calculates what your primary insurance amount will be, which your benefit is based on.

The formula requires 35 of your highest earning years. When you are finally at full retirement age, you will be able to draw 100% of that amount. If you were born in 1960 or later, your full retirement age is 67.

Once you know when you can retire at full retirement age, you can work out whether or not you want to receive a reduced benefit earlier (62), full benefit at 67, or an increased benefit by waiting until you are 70 years old.

The question then becomes, how much will you get at different ages? You need to know this so that you can decide how to take action. At full retirement age, you are eligible for your complete or "full" benefit provided that you have worked in a job that covers Social Security.

If you decide—out of need—that you want to take the benefit early, you will receive less than your full retirement age benefit. At age 62, you can expect to receive about 70% of full retirement age benefit. The reduction is permanent.

If you delay drawing your full Social Security benefit, you will increase your amount for every month that you do not draw. The benefits will increase by a predetermined percentage for every month, up until the age of 70.

If you were born in 1943, your Social Security will increase by 2/3 of 1%, or by 8% annually. If you were supposed to retire at 66, but wait until you are 70, you will receive benefits that are 32% higher than if you had drawn at full retirement age.

There are many benefit calculators that you can use with your spouse to help you determine the correct age at which to draw your Social Security benefits. Use them!

The Break-Even Work Decision

If you plan on working through your 60s and into your 70s to increase your retirement savings, you will need to know whether you can still draw on your Social Security to increase your monthly income.

Of course you can! A lot of people choose to apply for Social Security benefits before they actually retire. Many others still retire from full-time careers and switch to part-time work. If you want to increase your Social Security benefit, it will be beneficial to you to continue to work and earn income so that you can delay your withdrawal date.

The annual benefits increase each year as you work and add income to your total income earned during your lifetime. Even though you can work and still get Social Security, if you are younger than your projected full retirement age, your wages may temporarily reduce your benefit when you draw it out.

There is an annual earnings limit, and if your earnings exceed that amount, then part of your Social Security benefit will be withheld, reducing the amount that you get every month. Once you hit retirement age, you can work and collect—and your earnings will not affect your Social Security benefit.

Generally if you are 62 or under full retirement age and you earn, $1 of your benefit will be withheld for every $2 you earn over your annual earnings limit. A higher earnings limit will apply in the year you reach full retirement—$1 of your benefit will be withheld for every $3 you earn over $41,400.

If you are 63 years old, for example, and you started collecting Social Security and if you earn $10,000.00 more than the annual earnings limit of $15,480—$5,000.00 of that benefit will be withheld. That is $1 for every $2 above the earnings limit held.

Because of all of this, you need to know what your break-even age is. Calculating it will help you compare your long-term financial consequences of starting benefits at one age vs. another. You should reach your break-even age about 12 years after your full retirement age.

Your break-even age is the age at which the total value of your retirement benefits taken at one age is equal to the value of your benefits taken at a second age. Use this formula to determine how much you will get—or lose—each month. Factor it into your decision.

Taxed Benefits and Spouse Consideration

Depending on your income, taxes must be determined so that you can properly understand how Social Security will impact you and your spouse. If your only income during that year is from Social Security, then there will be no taxes.

For any other income that you bring in that same year, it may result in taxation of your Social Security benefit. You need to constantly be aware of how other sources of income are taxed to determine your authentic tax liability.

If you file as an "individual" and your combined income is...

- less than $25,000.00, you do not have to worry.
- between $25,000 and $34,000, you may have to pay income tax on up to 50% of your benefit.
- more than $34,000, up to 85% of your benefits may be taxable.

If you file "married filing jointly" and your combined income is...

- less than $32,000, you do not have to worry.
- between $32,000 and $44,000, you may have to pay income tax on up to 50% of your benefit.
- more than $44,000, up to 85% of your benefits may be taxable.

Quick calculation is this: your combined income is equal to your adjusted gross income + non-taxable income + ½ of Social Security benefit income = Your Combined Income.

When you are making your decision about when to begin receiving your Social Security benefits, keep federal and state taxable income in mind. Any earned income outside of your benefits may fall into the tax category, which could lower your overall income.

This decision affects your joint retirement plan, so it is essential that this decision is made as husband and wife. Find out if you are both eligible for benefits, how much each of you will receive, and what your combined life expectancies are.

Planning this together will open you up to specific retirement benefits based on your own and your spouse's earning record. Surviving spouses may qualify for widow or widower benefits based on what their partner was receiving.

It is good practice to find out what will happen if one of you passes away. The rules are generally straightforward: if your spouse did not work or had low income, they are entitled to 50% of your full retirement amount if their benefits begin at full retirement age.

If you are already receiving payments from your benefit, you can collect spousal benefits from the age of 62, though the amount will be permanently reduced. Plus, after full retirement age, the surviving spouse is eligible for 100% of their own benefit and 100% of what their spouse was earning at the time of their death.

The best way to navigate these eventualities is to contact the Social Security Administration online at **www.ssa.gov**, call them at 800-772-1213, or visit your local SSA office. There are lots of complicated rules that accompany spousal consideration, so make it clear in your mind before deciding on anything.

Planning Opportunities for Married Couples

As a married couple, there are many planning opportunities for you that will improve both of your Social Security retirement income results. Both can be used for a wide range of different scenarios; see which ones make the most sense to you.

- File and suspend: In Social Security, a husband or wife that can file for benefits based on their spouse's record cannot do so until they begin receiving their benefits. There is an exception, however—if you reach your full retirement age, you can choose to file for retirement benefits then request to have them suspended so that the eligible spouse can file for spousal benefits.

The old file and suspend option is a standard practice that occurs when one of the spouses had much lower lifetime earnings. They usually receive a higher retirement benefit based on their spouse's earning record rather than their own.

This opportunity can boost your retirement income in one of three main ways:

- The spouse with those higher earnings will suspend their benefits and accrue delayed retirement credit at a rate of 8% per year until age 70—thereby increasing their eventual payout by 32%.
- The spouse with those lower earnings will claim for the higher spousal retirement benefit and will get their partner's Social Security instead.
- The surviving spouse's benefit that is available to the lower-earning spouse will increase because they receive benefits equal to 100% of the monthly retirement benefit that the other spouse was getting at the time of their passing.

You can file for one benefit then another using a restricted application. Once you reach full retirement age and become eligible for a spousal benefit based on your spouse's earning record—and a retirement benefit based on your own earning record—you can choose to file a restricted application for spousal benefits.

Then you can delay filing for your own benefits up until you are 70 years old for additional Social Security credits. This will maximize your income and make sure that the surviving spouse is taken care of from both streams of income.

Retirement Pension vs. Social Security

Social Security was established as a way to prevent poverty in old age, and while it resembles a state pension, it is not anything like a retirement pension. If you have spent the last 30 years paying installments into a pension plan, then you will be granted a retirement pension by the financial institution that you chose.

Social Security, on the other hand, is really a social insurance program run by the United States Government. Unlike retirement plans, Social Security is not private or run by an independent financial institution.

Many of my clients ask me if having a retirement pension will affect the benefits that you stand to gain from Social Security. If your pension is from a job where you paid lots of Social Security taxes, then it will NOT be affected at all. Your Social Security benefit will remain intact.

If, however, your pension is from a job where you did NOT pay Social Security taxes, then two special provisions apply. These two provisions dictate how the two function together in these instances.

- The GPO, or government pension offset, could apply if you are set to receive a government pension as well as Social Security spousal retirement or survivor benefits based on your spouse's lifetime earnings. In this provision, your spousal benefit could be reduced by two-thirds of your government pension.

- The WEP, or windfall elimination provision, will affect how your Social Security retirement or disability benefit is calculated if you receive a pension from work that is not covered by Social Security. The formula finds out if your benefit needs to be changed, which sometimes results in lower Social Security payouts.

Except for these two instances, it is fairly safe to say that your corporate or private retirement pension will not impact your Social Security benefit at all.

Changing Your Mind About Social Security Benefits

I have mentioned on more than one occasion here that once you begin your Social Security withdrawals, that is it. The decision is permanent and cannot be revoked. Except in certain circumstances!

That said, you do have a limited opportunity to change your mind once you have applied for your Social Security benefits. Simply complete Form SSA-521, which is a request for withdrawal of your application form—and then you can reapply at a later time or date.

If you are already receiving benefits, you can only withdraw your claim if it has been less than 12 months since you first became entitled to benefits. You may only get one withdrawal per lifetime. That means you can take your benefits then change your mind a total of ONCE before it becomes a hard and unchangeable scenario.

You will also have to endure financial consequences of this "false start," and you will have to repay all benefits that have been paid out to you or your family members, based on your application. This includes money withheld from your checks, Medicare premiums, and tax withholding.

All in all, it is quite a mission to decide to withdraw from your Social Security benefits. Not only do you have to pay back everything they gave you, but it can cost you money in fees and expenses sorting out the paperwork and dealing with your financial advisor.

There are often unexpected changes in life, so you can never tell how you will need to behave in future situations. That is why it is good to understand that changing your mind is an option, though not a very good one.

Proper planning and strategy with your retirement portfolio will ensure that you do not ever have to change your mind because you will need the money when you are older. An application withdraw is really like a reset.

You give everything back, and they reset the clock. It works, but it is a financial hassle for you. Everyone who receives benefits in your household will have to consent to the withdrawal of your application for Social Security until a later date.

CHAPTER 11

Power of Roth IRA Conversion

"Retirement has been a discovery of beauty for me.
I never had the time before to notice the beauty of my
grandkids, my wife, the tree outside my very own front
door, and the beauty of time itself."

HARTMAN JULE

It is day 9, and that means you are nearing the end of your 10-day retirement planning blueprint. In this section, I am going to explain Roth conversions to you and why they are important to consider.

By choosing to do a Roth conversion, you can put yourself in a better financial place than before within your retirement portfolio.

The Roth IRA Conversion Changes

In the years before 2010, you were only able to convert a traditional IRA to a Roth IRA or get an ERD (eligible rollover distribution) from your employer plan to a Roth IRA under two key circumstances.

The first was if you modified your gross income and it did not exceed $100,000; the second was if your filing status could not be married filing separately. After 2010 these status requirements for Roth conversions were eliminated!

The new rules state that it does not matter what your income or filing status might be; you are able to roll over or convert any of the following into a Roth IRA.

- A SIMPLE IRA, SEP IRA, or a traditional IRA
- An ERD from your retirement (like your 401k or 403b plan)
- An ERD from a retirement plan that you are the beneficiary for

You can still make contributions up to $5,500.00 to your Roth IRA in 2014. If you are 50 or older, you will be able to contribute that extra thousand at $6,500.00. Keep in mind that your contributions cannot exceed your annual taxable compensation. Review chapter 4 for the contribution eligibility.

Converting From Traditional to ROTH IRA

There are lots of ways that you can now convert your traditional IRA to a Roth IRA. Of them, there are three that make the most sense:

- You can engage in a rollover. This is when you will receive a distribution from your traditional IRA and then "roll it over" to your Roth IRA within 60 days—once the distribution has been processed.
- You can conduct a trustee-to-trustee transfer if you direct the trustee of the traditional IRA to transfer an amount from your traditional IRA to the trustee of your Roth IRA.
- You can also conduct a "same trustee" transfer. If the trustee of your traditional IRA also happens to maintain your Roth IRA, you can direct them to transfer your amount from your traditional IRA to your Roth IRA.

Required minimum distributions cannot be rolled over, as a general rule. If you are going to convert your traditional IRA to a Roth IRA, these considerations must be met.

Calculating the Conversion Tax

Whenever a traditional IRA to Roth IRA conversion is made, you will be taxed that same year as if you had made a withdrawal from your traditional IRA.

Everything will be the same except for one big difference—the 10% early distribution penalty tax does not apply to Roth conversions even if you have not yet reached the age of 59 and a half.

If you do decide to make a non-qualified withdrawal of converted funds from your Roth IRA, within five years of the conversion the IRS can recapture those early distribution penalties.

If you only have deductible contributions to your traditional IRA, then calculating tax is easy. Your whole amount will be subject to federal income tax. If you have made non-deductible, or after tax, contributions to your traditional IRA, it gets a bit more complicated.

These non-deductible contributions mean that any time you take a distribution, your withdrawal is treated like a pro-rata amount of taxable and non-taxable dollars. Conversions are taxed just like withdrawals are, so the same rules apply!

You cannot convert just the non-taxable portion of your traditional IRA in order to end up with a tax-free conversion. Plus, when you take a withdrawal from any traditional IRA that you own, you have to aggregate that particular IRA with any other IRAs that you own.

This means you need to combine your SEP and SIMPLE IRAs when you work out what your taxable and non-taxable areas of your withdrawal are. It applies to conversions!

You may not just transfer the non-taxable portion of your traditional IRA to a separate IRA then convert that new IRA to a Roth in order to avoid all conversion taxes. At some point, these taxes will have to be paid.

Roth Conversions with Little or No Taxes

Obviously, every situation is unique. However, you could convert your IRA/401k to a Roth IRA and pay very little or no taxes during the conversion year. Let me share with you three hypotheticals:

1. Let's pretend that you own your own business and file Schedule C on your Federal Form 1040, and you project that you will have a significant loss of $50,000 for that year.

Also, let's pretend that your spouse does not work. You could convert $50,000 of your IRA to a Roth IRA and pay $0 income tax because the $50,000 loss will offset your $50,000 taxable income from the conversion.

2. You recently retired, and you are living off of your investment accounts before you start collecting on Social Security or pension income. Your income may be low enough to convert some of your IRA to a Roth IRA and still pay very little or no taxes on the conversion.

3. You currently have 401k/403b or other employer-sponsored retirement accounts. However, you have no IRA, SIMPLE IRA, or SEP IRA. Also, your earned income is above the phase-out (see chapter 4). Therefore, you cannot make any direct contribution to your Roth IRA. You can still establish an IRA first and make up to $5,500 (or $6,500) as a non-deductible contribution. Then, convert it to a Roth IRA. Since you did not make a deductible contribution, theoretically you could convert all of it in a tax-free conversion.

The key is to proactively review your tax situation and convert it to a Roth IRA during the calendar year (between January and December). Simply, you cannot convert in January 2015 and count it for 2014.

Can You Undo a Conversion?

Obviously, working with conversions can be difficult, which is why it is good to know that if you make a Roth conversion and it does not go as planned, you can always take steps to correct your mistake.

If the value of your Roth IRA drops, for example, once your conversion changes, then you can consider undoing the action.

Formally, this is called a recharacterization, but all it means is that you have chosen to UNDO the conversion you made to your Roth IRA.

It applies to the amounts that you will convert from a traditional IRA and amounts that you roll over from other employer-based plans. Generally, you have until the due date to file your tax return so that you can undo or recharacterize the conversion.

Here is an example—if you convert a traditional IRA to a Roth IRA in 2014, you will have until October 15, 2015 to recharacterize the conversion.

If you do, the amount that you converted plus any earnings on top of that is transferred into a traditional IRA—and the Roth conversion is treated as if it did not happen, for tax purposes.

If you like, you can reconvert your traditional IRA back into a Roth once you have satisfied the waiting period—which can sometimes be as quick as 30 days.

Is Your Roth Conversion a Good Fit?

You agree by now that Roth IRAs are excellent retirement savings plans. But is a conversion the best thing for you? The answer depends on your goals and your unique situation.

Converting makes a lot of sense if you believe that you will be in a higher tax bracket in the future, when you start taking your distributions.

All qualified distributions are tax-free, which means that you will be able to supplement any taxable income that you may have with the tax-free income that will not impact the taxation of your Social Security benefits or any other tax benefits that affect your adjusted gross income.

Another argument for converting would be that you are required to take distributions from your traditional IRA when you are 70 and a half. With Roth IRAs, you do not have to draw from them during your lifetime. It can literally sit, compounding tax-free for longer periods of time. Leaving more money to your heirs can be done this way.

If I was to argue against a Roth conversion, I would say this—if you are expecting to be in a lower tax bracket in the future, when you will begin taking your distributions, then conversion does not make sense. However, there is no guarantee that the government will have the same current tax bracket.

You will have to pay federal income tax on all or part of the amount that you choose to convert. If you have to use IRA dollars to pay the conversion tax, the benefits are significantly reduced.

Using IRA money to pay taxes will reduce the lump sum in your fund, which could jeopardize your retirement goals. The IRA money that you would use to pay the taxes could also be subject to tax—income tax and a potential distribution penalty tax.

Any income you draw before you are eligible for tax-free qualified distributions will be taxed, and the IRS will take the penalty taxes you should have paid on conversion.

CHAPTER 12

Seeking Your Personal Financial Coach

"The only way you will ever permanently take control of your financial life is to dig deep and fix the root problem."

SUZE ORMAN

You have reached the final day of this retirement blueprint, and day 10 means discussing the possibility of sourcing and hiring a personal financial planner.

Your main goal in this section is to come to terms with the idea that your retirement portfolio is fairly complex to manage, and having a good financial planner on your side can make all of the difference in the long term.

Why Should You Use a Financial Planner?

There are lots of reasons why you should consider hiring a financial advisor to help you make the right decisions about your retirement portfolio.

- A competent financial planner should be your direct line to sound financial planning advice that suits your goals and directives.
- Sometimes taking control of your financial future means enlisting the help of someone who has a little more insight into the world of finance than you do.
- When you have lots of questions—and need solid answers—that is a good time to consider finding a financial planner for your portfolio.

- If you have come into a lot of money recently and are not sure how to use it to secure your retirement one day, a financial planner is a wise option.

- If you are having trouble achieving your financial goals on your own, then this may also be a great time to suggest chatting to a financial advisor.

The short answer is that if you are serious about making the right decisions with money, then you should use a financial planner to confirm your own research and decisions in finance.

What to Look For in a Financial Planner

Financial planners should never lead you to your decisions; they should act as advisors or guides, adding in expert commentary on vehicles and processes that you are already entirely aware of, or you will end up in the dark about your own portfolio.

To prevent this from happening, you need to know what to look for in a financial planner. Follow these basic rules for best results:

- Look for a financial planner that has at least a CFP® certificate (Certified Financial Planner). They have to go through a very strict national exam that certifies them to create financial plans, so you know they will be capable of it.

- Financial planners should take your personal life into account—they should not just recommend products to you based on what kind of financial future you want. This is how you end up with an unregulated, poorly contrived portfolio.

- Make sure that you like your financial planner and that there is good communication between the two of you or between you as a couple and the advisor.

- Ask to hear about, see, and chat to their past clients. You will want to know how they operate, what they are able to achieve, and where their strengths and weaknesses lie.

- Also ask them about if they had any customer/client complaints that you should be aware of. (See next section on performing background checks)

Financial planners should not be pushy or take a hard line with you about your planning. It is great to be passionate, but ultimately where they steer you will determine how you are able to retire in your old age, and that is perhaps the most important thing in your life.

Performing Background Checks

Did you know that the bulk of people investigate or perform background checks on their financial planners, brokers, and advisors? This is because there are a lot of poor practices in the industry that can cost you your life savings.

Even worse than that, there are practices in the industry that will result in you having nothing when you turn 62, even if you thought you had a comprehensive portfolio. That is why it is critical to concentrate on thoroughly investigating your planner before you hire them.

- *Visit http://brokercheck.finra.org to conduct a FINRA broker check on your planner.*

Here, the information about investment advisor firms and representatives that is made available through the Brokercheck site is taken from the Securities and Exchange Commission's Investment Advisor Public Disclosure database.

The IAPD, as it is called, actually features professional background information on approximately 441,000 current and former investment advisor representatives and 45,700 current and former investment advisor firms.

More detailed information about those firms and representatives can be obtained via the provided hyperlinks on the IAPD website. I suggest you visit there today and have a look around.

It is always a good idea to perform a background check on your financial advisor to make sure that their qualifications, standards, and integrity are transparent.

What to Look For During These Checks

There are lots of different types of financial planners that you can choose from, but the one that is going to look after your interests the best is the independent advisor.

Gone are the days of staying with the first financial planner that you find. Your investment choices are extremely complex and carry heavy ramifications, so selecting the wrong planner will impact your retirement so negatively that it is not something you can afford to do.

Consider an independent financial planner that is not associated with a bank, insurance, or wire house. Depending on who they are associated with, their interests may not be in line with yours. I am not saying that all planners with those other associations are a bad fit. However, they may be dealing with their own minimum revenue or sales quotas from the company they work for. I personally used to work for a big insurance company and bank in the past. It is purely my personal experience with them.

This makes it possible for them to align with your needs instead of placing corporate needs above your end goals.

You should aim to find a smart, independent broker that is successful financially in his or her own right. They need to be family-orientated and willing to get to know you and your specific needs as a client. If they are only about the money, then they are not of any real help.

What Kind of Planner Do You Choose?

It can be tough finding a planner that fits in with your lifestyle and that is easy to communicate with on an ongoing basis. But that is exactly what you need to do. The kind of planner that you choose will determine the kind of retirement portfolio you are able to put together.

That is why you need to screen them by asking any number of the following strict questions:

- How do you charge for your services?
- How much are your services?
- What are your payment structures (and do they suit you)?
- What licenses, credentials, and other certifications do you have?
- What types of clients do you specialize in?
- Ask to see several examples of your planner's financial plans.
- What is your investment approach?
- How much contact do you have with your clients?
- Will I be working with you or with your team?
- What makes your client experience unique and valuable?
- Have you ever been involved in a client dispute?
- How did you clear up your client dispute?
- Have you ever filed for bankruptcy for a client?

You can add to this question list as much as you like. The point is that by the end of these questions, you have a better understanding of who your financial planner is as an advisor and as a human being.

There is no one-size-fits-all solution in the financial world, which is why choosing your planner can be so difficult. If you interview several advisors—or take on more than one—you will have a better understanding of how to navigate the investment landscape simply based on how they respond to your questions and interests in investing.

Financial Planners: They Are All Different

All financial planners are different, and even though you can assume that the corporate types have their companies' best interests in mind, the same can be true for independent brokers out to make their fortune with other people's money.

There are a vast majority of honest and reliable planners out there, but as in every industry, the ones that are bad, or negligent, or selfish give everyone else a terrible name. Just because they are licensed, they believe they can get away with any number of bad, fee-producing investments that will produce lots of commission for them.

Because all planners are different, you need to assume that YOU are the guardian of your own retirement portfolio and that an advisor is there to confirm or dispel information based on knowledge that you already have.

It is a sad truth that some 70% of people do not do background checks on their financial planners. Handing over the decisions for your life savings to a total stranger needs to be taken more seriously—they are just people after all.

Your financial planner, above all, needs to fit with your ideologies and lifestyle. They must be certified and well-practiced and have a great reputation among their existing clients. A FINRA broker check will help you sort through the rest.

On those background websites, often all you have to do is submit a name, and you will be sent a PDF document detailing information about that planner. This is a great starting point for hiring.

Do not make assumptions about your independent financial planner, rather test them out. Assume that they have to prove to you that they are who they say they are and can achieve what they promise you. If they fail you on this, chat about it; if you leave, it does not get resolved. There are no friends in the investment business. Money talks.

CHAPTER 13

Asking the
Right Financial
Questions

"Academic qualifications are important and so is
financial education. They're both important and
schools are forgetting one of them."

ROBERT KIYOSAKI

You are in the second leg of your final day, and this is where you will go a little deeper into how to hire the right financial planner. I cannot stress enough how pivotal this is to your eventual retirement portfolio.

Each box must be checked so that you end up with a reliable, responsible, and trustworthy financial planner that will help set you up with an ideal retirement scenario.

Charging for Services Rendered

The very first concern that you have to consider when hiring a financial planner is their fee structure. Payments are a key part of financial planning, and as an informed investor, you want to make sure that you fully understand all fees, expenses, and commissions.

Otherwise, you will end up with unexpected fees and payment structures that you did not agree to. Your financial planner needs to be receptive to an interview so that you can ask them the right questions about how they will be paid.

There are dozens of arrangements that you can make on how to pay a financial planner. Fee-only planners charge by the hour, though they could also bill a percentage of your investment assets if you place them on retainer.

If you need your financial planner to design your retirement portfolio for you or manage your mutual funds on an ongoing basis, they may also require a retainer. Then there are others that charge a combination of fees and commissions.

You MUST request a written breakdown of all payment structures so that you are not surprised to find that your broker has earned incredible sums of money off your portfolio in a few years' time.

You should also ask how these structures are determined, which ones are fixed, and which ones are variable. Then you can take them and compare them with other financial planners' fee structures to benchmark if you are being given a fair price. Pay as you go is generally the best way to handle and pay your financial planner.

Searching for Licenses, Credentials, and Certifications

You would not trust a doctor to remove an organ if they did not study for 10 years first and have the kind of job that constantly forced them to improve their practical skills. The same can be assumed of a financial advisor.

Typically, you need to establish their level of education and what kind of additional credentials or licenses they have. The most basic is, of course, the Certified Financial Planner (CFP®) credential because it is highly regulated.

Financial planners with this qualification have to take a series of courses and then pass a very serious, two-day, 10-part exam. There is a minimum of three years' work experience that is required in order for a CFP® to be awarded.

That is why when you hire a financial planner that is CFP® certified, you are guaranteed the kind of education and practical application that someone in investment needs to make good decisions for you.

Then there is the wonderful 30 hours of mandatory continued education that all financial planners must complete every two years to maintain their credential. This ensures that they remain up-to-date on the latest financial trends and, as such, are better equipped to inform you about any policy or government changes.

I suggest that in the interview, you sit down with your financial planner and discuss their credentials and certifications in detail. Then, once they have left, verify each credential with the appropriate body. You will be surprised how easy it is to claim to be a member of an association when there is no real affiliation there.

Service Profile and Client Specialization

A great financial planner should truly understand that you have a right to know exactly what kind of services he is offering and why. If they are working to sell someone's services or specific funds, then you need to know about that.

Their job is to provide you with recommendations based on your personal financial profile and needs, not on hidden agendas that they have. This includes conducting data gathering on your personal financial situation, analyzing this data, and then making recommendations based on their extensive experience and your wishes.

That means you need to know about all of the services that they offer and how their method of recommendation might affect your eventual portfolio. The best financial planners in the industry are the ones that offer client specializations.

This is when they pick a niche to specialize in and stick to it—instead of trying to be everything to all of their clients. What you are looking for is a financial planner that specializes in retirement portfolio creation and management.

If you purposefully search for one with this specialization, you will end up gaining detailed knowledge from an expert in this niche area as you are putting together your portfolio. The other end of this decision is to take on a financial planner that does not specialize—and knows almost as much as you do about retirement planning.

Building on a specific type of expertise results in the kind of in-depth knowledge that will help you avoid major pitfalls and include little-known provisions or changes to your portfolio that may make all the difference one day.

I believe as a couple, it is your job to find a financial advisor that can offer you the kind of client specialization that you deserve. Match that with the right service profile and transparency that stimulates trust, and you are onto something.

Sample Financial Plans and Investment Approaches

There are some investment approaches that you want to watch out for when hiring your financial planner. You should also be able to request specific sample financial plans that they can work through with you so that you better understand how they work and what their investment style may be.

Initially, you need to explore how they approach retirement investment, in a fairly thorough manner. Ask them about their past clients, beliefs, and experience, and see how often they recommend certain courses of action.

Keep in mind that you are the most knowledgeable person at the end of the day and that your planner is just a coach to enhance your personal retirement decisions. That said, they need to have access to a network of other experts so that if they need to check on something, they can.

It is very beneficial to have a financial planner that is highly involved in the niche and has access to different types of financial experts. They should be able to demonstrate who they know and how they use these connections to enhance their own client portfolios.

Once you have run through your financial planner's cost structures, credentials, services, and specializations, the next logical step is to check out the way they approach their new investment portfolios. If you like it, it may be a good match.

If you find the process disjointed, too conservative, too aggressive, or not in line with your own ideas, you can discuss it with them and decide on whether the relationship is worth pursuing.

It is far better for you financially to pick out a good financial coach early than to have to "break up" with a hastily chosen one later on. This can often be expensive and a little messy. Gather the sample plans and approaches and review them together.

Contact and Team Dynamics

The next step is to review how they plan on working with you through your retirement investment process. Some financial planners have a specific style that they apply to their customer care, so you need to know about that.

- *How will your financial coach communicate with you? How often? Will you be in constant contact, or do they prefer a more hands-off approach?*

If you are the kind of person who likes to call your financial planner often, then make sure you find one who is always available for that. If you are happy simply receiving monthly reports after your initial consultations, then find an advisor who suits that.

The way you will communicate with and contact your planner will determine how good your relationship stays and how informed you are about your retirement portfolio. Do not underestimate the power of having a friendly planner on your side.

Once this is sorted out, you can question your planner on their team. Sometimes a company will send you a financial advisor, but really, their team will be doing most of the work. You end up being passed from one person to the next and barely even see your advisor most of the time. I know many people that will not tolerate that.

Instead, make it clear that you do not mind working with teams as long as you are properly introduced to them and can also run background checks on them. It is nothing personal, but if someone is going to be handling your account, you should want to make sure that they are at least capable of doing that.

The couples that are most certain about what they want from their financial coach usually get the best returns. They seek out a particular kind of person, hold them accountable, and a high level of trust is developed between them.

Digging a Little Deeper: Experience

As I was saying earlier, in the finance field, practical application is the real evidence that someone knows what they are doing. The very last thing you need to check up on is the kind of experience that your financial coach has had.

Your aim is to establish a long-term relationship with a great financial planner that will help you make consistently accurate investment decisions based on your needs. The quickest way to see if this is possible from their side is to check on their experience.

- How long have they been working? In the financial space? In a niche financial area? Do not be afraid to ask prying questions.
- Who have they worked for, and do they have any success stories that can be verified?
- Can you take a look at any data from past client experiences?
- Can you chat to at least three of their past clients so that you can get a better feel for the way they work and who they are?

- Check on their actual title—are they a CFP (Certified Financial Planner, CPA (Certified Public Accountant, etc.

- Speak with them at length about their investment philosophy. If you have two opposing ideas, your relationship is never going to work out.

If you can profile who their typical client is, then you will easily be able to see who fits in best with their level of experience and expertise. When you take the time as a couple to dig a little deeper into who you are hiring to help you with your money, it always pays off.

CHAPTER 14

Federal Tax Reduction Strategies

"I am proud to be paying taxes in the United States. The only thing is I could be just as proud for half of the money."

ARTHUR GODFREY

You have achieved something great over the last 10 days, so to show my appreciation, I am adding in this bonus chapter to educate you on tax reduction.

Do not discount the fact that taxes play a very big role in retirement portfolio building and managing, so it helps to take a bird's eye view of the issue.

What Are Federal Tax Reductions?

Everyone hates the tax system, but it is here to stay, and it exists for very good reasons. In business and in your personal life, you will be dealing with taxes up until the day you retire and then some form of taxes after that.

Tax planning should always be "top of mind" for your financial coach, as the ability to find and secure tax breaks or leverage tax reduction benefits goes a long way to saving you money during your life-long retirement portfolio creation process.

Federal tax reductions are either tax credits or income tax deductions that you get if you make provision for investing in certain financial plans, like your 401k. The federal government tries to make it easier to save as a couple by allowing you certain breaks if you contribute to your retirement.

A good example is the tax-free Roth IRA. In this instance, the federal government will not tax your Roth savings until you withdraw the money on retirement. Because of this, it is allowed to grow with compound interest, tax-free, over time—which is very beneficial for you.

How Your Taxes Can Be Minimized

Of course, to take advantage of federal tax reductions, you need to know how, or where, they exist. Your financial planner and the two of you as a couple should explore this element of your retirement portfolio as well as you can.

The amount of taxes that you pay is not a fixed amount. Everyone that gets the same income does not pay the same in taxes. It is awise to explore financial strategy to minimize your taxes, which means that you need to be informed about the laws, regulations, and court decisions that have been issued as a guidance tool.

Federal, state, and local government bodies are considered your partner—they will dip into your income and set the rules for how much money they are owed. Taking advantage of legitimate outs and reliefs is an excellent way to maximize your portfolio.

Easing your tax load is important if you want your retirement to be everything you dreamed of and more. Adjusting your taxes up or down is a key element in controlling the outcomes of your retirement portfolio. As in business, learning how to utilize tax will greatly benefit you over time.

Knowing the tax status of your investments, for example, can lead to you leveraging these reductions in order to make more profit at the right time. Tax should also be seen as something that helps you make a decision to buy or invest in something.

You should also fully understand the tax implications of any fund, account, or policy that you open. Sometimes tweaking the tax can save you thousands of dollars every year, if you know where to nip and tuck!

The Difference Between Ordinary vs. Qualified Dividends

In the realm of understanding what happens with tax at every investment level, there are ordinary and qualified dividends. If you own business stocks or have invested in mutual funds, you will start receiving dividend payments at specified times during the year.

The companies that pay these dividends to you will also send you reports on your payments, which will detail how much of them are qualified dividends. Tax varies depending on your type of dividend, so knowing the difference between one or the other is very important.

- *An ordinary dividend*: These payments are received on your earnings or profit from a corporation or mutual fund that you have chosen to invest in. If you own tech stocks, for example, that company can choose to pay their shareholders dividends because of a great financial year. Ordinary dividend tax rules apply in this instance.

- *A qualified divided*: These dividends are really a subtype of ordinary dividends that are subject to some great tax rules that can work to save you a ton of money on your tax return. So while qualified dividends are ordinary, not all ordinary dividends are qualified.

To be a qualified dividend, the company that pays out must be a U.S. corporation, or a company that has been incorporated into U.S. possession, or a foreign company that has a tax treaty with the U.S.

These dividend payments are taxed at a maximum of 20%, whereas other types of ordinary dividends can be taxed as high as 39.6%. Sometimes, in special circumstances, the tax payer does not have to pay any tax at all on their qualified dividends.

Capital Gains: Short and Long Term

Also in the realm of taxation lie capital gains. The IRS has always taxed different income at different a tes. Ca pital g ins from something like the profit earned from the sale of stock is usually taxed at a lower rate than income/salary.

No two capital gains are the same, however—and tax does tend to vary radically between short-term and long-term gains. Generating gains—for example, in your retirement account will affect your overall tax rate.

- *A short-term capital gain*: These tend not to benefit from special tax rates, and they are usually taxed at the same rate as your monthly income. The tax ranges from 10 to 39.6% depending on the total amount of taxable income that you earn. Selling an asset you have owned for less than a year is a short-term capital gain.

- *Long- term capital gain*: Hanging onto your assets for a longer period of time means that you will be able to benefit from reduced tax rates on your profit. A long-term capital gain tax rate is about 0–20% for most people, depending on your asset.

With retirement accounts especially, you can defer on paying taxes on any gains in an IRA, for example, which is hugely beneficial for long-term growth.

The catch, of course, is that once the money has grown and you need to draw it out, all money taken from your IRA is taxable as ordinary income. The initial tax-deferred status is the only benefit, which helps getting couples like you off the mark with retirement savings.

Starting a Business?

The way that businesses are organized makes a difference in the tax world, so pay attention if you plan on starting a business anytime soon. Tax often determines whether a company will become a close corporation, an incorporated business, or something else.

Federal laws and regulations change all the time, and this will impact your business down the line. Whether your business is started as a small business or a large one also matters.

- For S corporations, there are lots of tax benefits and disadvantages. For example, it is great that profit is not taxed until it is paid to shareholders. If you choose to form a C corporation, you could be taxed as much as 35% of corporate income. Corporate tax starts at 15% on your first $50,000. Losing that much money to tax is a reality, and one you should consider.

There are some business models that always pay the flat 35% tax— doctors, accountants, and law firms tend to do that. Accumulated earnings tax is also something that occurs in a corporation, where the IRS takes 20% of any excess earnings left in your company.

There are, however, dozens of ways to avoid the accumulated earnings tax, just like there are ways to minimize the disadvantages of owning a corporation—which, as any advisor will tell you, is the most sensible tax-based business model.

Explore the various forms of business and decide how best to utilize tax to maximize profit for your business. There are many different types of business within the corporation model, so do not be too hasty to avoid it. In short, consult a qualified tax advisor or attorney for what type of business entity you should start.

Having a Health Savings Account

Another type of account you and your spouse should consider for tax purposes is a health savings account. Increasingly, employers are offering high-deductible health insurance plans—which are not ideal and should be supported by a health savings account.

If your plan has no HSA, you can take one out with your financial planner. What it is, is a tax-free account that will help you if you need money for medical costs and expenses. You will place money into your HSA before it is taxed, and it will grow in that account tax-deferred; it is ALSO completely tax-free when you draw it out to use.

That means you can safely save for medical emergencies without having to worry about paying huge amounts to the tax man. When you do not have to pay tax to deposit, grow, or withdraw your money, you get a lot more compound interest happening, which is very beneficial for your family.

That way if your health plan has expenses that are not covered—or if there are wide gaps—you will be able to cover them based on your tax-free HSA account. The funny thing is that HSAs also have the ability to boost your retirement savings!

After the age of 65, you are completely free to draw money from your HSA, and you do not have to spend that money on medical expenses. So it becomes a way of saving and supplementing your retirement portfolio.

You must not confuse an HSA with an FSA—or a flexible spending account—as a lot of people do this, but they are both very different from each other. To get your HSA, you cannot, however, be enrolled in a Medicare program.

Signing up for one is easy, and you can place up to $3,300.00 in your account each year or $6,550.00 if you are on a family plan. If you begin at age 30, thirty years of contribution could mount to $196,500 before adding any interest.

Conclusion

You have completed your 10-day retirement blueprint, and now you are completely ready to sit down with the financial coach of your choice and get to work.

Retirement planning has always been seen as a hassle, but when you have the right information and the right guidance, creating your personalized retirement portfolio can make you and your spouse feel more confident in the knowledge that when old age comes, you will be ready financially.

I would encourage you to work through this program once or twice to really absorb the key pieces of knowledge that will help you make the right decisions about your financial future when you reach your twilight years.

From planning your ideal retirement to learning how to save and make the right investment vehicle choices, I hope I have given you the tools that you needed to make educated decisions when you finally sit down with your financial coach.

Retirement does not have to be something that you dread. It can be a time that you look forward to, work towards, and deserve with some careful planning and strategy. When you spend your whole life working hard, there is nothing more rewarding than retiring with a lifestyle that you love and money in your pocket to enjoy your remaining years.

Do not allow the complexity or density of financial topics to steer your attention away from what matters. It is up to you as a couple to prepare for your future. I have given you the valuable tools to do this; now it is up to you.

Retire in paradise,

Sunwook Jin

References

Chapter 1

Retirement Quotes, Brainyquote, http://www.brainyquote.com/quotes/keywords/retirement.html

Deveau, Denise, *The Big Retirement Question: How Much Do I Need To Save?,* http://business.financialpost.com/2014/01/20/the-big-retirement-question-how-much-do-i-need-to-save/

O'Hara, Carolyn, *10 Retirement Misconceptions That Could Derail Your Golden Years,* http://www.forbes.com/sites/learnvest/2014/01/23/10-retirement-misconceptions-that-could-derail-your-golden-years/

Udo, Joe, *Build Your Own Retirement Plan,* http://money.usnews.com/money/blogs/On-Retirement/2013/08/01/build-your-own-retirement-plan

Four Steps To Building a Retirement Plan You Can Count On, http://www.northwesternmutual.com/learning-center/article-library/building-retirement-plan.aspx

Lawler, Jennifer, *3 Ways To Build a Secure Retirement Plan,* http://www.bankrate.com/finance/retirement/3-ways-to-build-a-secure-retirement-plan-1.aspx

Herigstad, Sally, *6 Surprising IRA Investment Options,* http://www.bankrate.com/finance/retirement/6-surprising-ira-investment-options-1.aspx

Retirement Planning 101: Understanding Investment Options, http://www.mymax.com/learn-and-plan/retirement-planning-101-understanding-investment-options.html

Berger, Robert, *6 Options For Boosting Your Yield in Retirement,* http://money.usnews.com/money/blogs/On-Retirement/2013/07/26/6-options-for-boosting-your-yield-in-retirement

Hamm, Trent, *Retirement: What's The Best Investment Option?,* http://www.csmonitor.com/Business/The-Simple-Dollar/2012/0629/Retirement-What-s-the-best-investment-option

Scherzer, Lisa, *How Much Do You Need To Save For Retirement?,* http://finance.yahoo.com/news/how-much-do-you-need-to-save-for-retirement-155348899.html

Anspach, Dana, *How Much Money To Retire? Calculate The Gap,* http://moneyover55.about.com/od/preretirementplanning/a/calculate_gap.htm

Estimating Your Retirement Income Needs, http://www.ameriprise.com/budgeting-investing/financial-planning-articles/retirement-planning-information/retirement-income-needs.asp

Chapter 2

Retirement Quotes, Brainyquote, http://www.brainyquote.com/quotes/keywords/retirement.html

Brandon, Emily, *10 Essential Sources of Retirement Income,* http://money.usnews.com/money/retirement/slideshows/10-essential-sources-of-retirement-income/11

Powell, Robert, *Will You Need 135% of Your Salary in Retirement?* http://www.marketwatch.com/story/will-you-need-135-of-your-salary-in-retirement-2011-09-08

Ruiz-Menjivar, Jorge, Gillen, Martie, *Retirement Need Analysis: How Much of My Current Income Will I Need For Retirement?*, http://edis.ifas.ufl.edu/fy1355

Projected Retirement Expense, http://ctainvest.org/home/calculators/expense-calculator.aspx

Rubin, Michael, *Top Steps Before You Retire, Part 2 – Evaluate Your Projected Retirement Cash Flow*, http://retireplan.about.com/od/howtobegin/a/topstep2.htm

Retirement Rules of Thumb, http://www.360financialliteracy.org/Topics/Retirement-Planning/Retirement-Planning-Basics/Retirement-Rules-of-Thumb

Uren, Adam, *New State Pension Age: As We're Told To Work Longer, When Will You Be Able To Retire?*, http://www.thisismoney.co.uk/money/pensions/article-1679780/New-state-pension-age-retire.html

Riggio, Dr Ronald, *At What Age Should You Retire?*, http://www.psychologytoday.com/blog/cutting-edge-leadership/201104/what-age-should-you-retire

Novack, Janet, *Essential Number For Retirement Planning: Your Personal Life Expectancy*, http://www.forbes.com/sites/janetnovack/2014/01/21/an-essential-number-for-retirement-planning-your-personal-life-expectancy/

Closing A Retirement Income Gap, http://www.ameriprise.com/budgeting-investing/financial-planning-articles/retirement-planning-information/retirement-income-shortfall.asp

A Blueprint For Retirement Income, http://www.liberty.edu/ media/1312/hr_formsmanager_forms/A%20Blueprint%20 for%20Retirement%20Income_Liberty%20University.pdf

Retirement Handbook, http://atyourservice.ucop.edu/forms_pubs/ misc/retirebook.pdf

Chapter 3

Retirement Quotes, Brainyquote, http://www.brainyquote.com/ quotes/keywords/retirement.html

Saving For Retirement – Options Other Than a Pension, http://www. moneysupermarket.com/savings/saving-for-retirement-guide/

Udo, Joe, *How To Save More For Retirement In 2014,* http://money. usnews.com/money/blogs/on-retirement/2014/01/09/how-to- save-more-for-retirement-in-2014

Geary, Leslie, *Retirement Planning For 20 Somethings,* http://www. bankrate.com/finance/financial-literacy/retirement-planning-for- 20-somethings-1.aspx

Chapter 4

Quotes About Retirement Planning, http://www.goodreads.com/ quotes/tag/retirement-planning#

Traditional IRA, Investopedia, http://www.investopedia.com/ terms/t/traditionalira.asp

Roth IRA, Investopedia, http://www.investopedia.com/terms/r/ rothira.asp

What Is The Difference Between a Traditional IRA and a Roth IRA, http://www.retire.prudential.com/view/page/rs/17022

Spors, Kelly, *Traditional IRA vs. Roth IRA*, http://www.rothira. com/traditional-ira-vs-roth-ira

Guina, Ryan, *Comparing Roth IRA Versus Traditional IRA*, http://cashmoneylife.com/traditional-ira-vs-roth-ira/

Kennan, Mark, *A Traditional IRA: Pros & Cons*, http://finance.zacks.com/traditional-ira-pros-cons-3801.html

Malone, Matthew, *What Is a Roth IRA?*, http://www.rothira.com/what-is-a-Roth-IRA

McCormally, Kevin, *Why You Need a Roth IRA*, http://www.kiplinger.com/article/retirement/T046-C006-S001-why-you-need-a-roth-ira.html

Chapter 5

Quotations: Retirement, http://www.quotegarden.com/retirement.html

What Is a 401K, http://guides.wsj.com/personal-finance/retirement/what-is-a-401k/

What Is a 401K Plan?, http://www.practicalmoneyskills.com/personalfinance/lifeevents/benefits/401k.php

401K Plan, Investopedia, http://www.investopedia.com/terms/1/401kplan.asp

Individual Retirement Annuity, http://www.investopedia.com/terms/i/individual_retirement_annuity.asp

Pavia, Jim, *Do Annuities Fit In a Retirement Plan?*, http://www.cnbc.com/id/101068618

What Is an Annuity?, http://money.cnn.com/retirement/guide/annuities_basics.moneymag/

Orman, Suze, *Annuities*, http://apps.suzeorman.com/igsbase/igs-template.cfm?SRC=MD012&SRCN=aoedetails&GnavID=84&SnavID=29&TnavID&AreasofExpertiseID=107

Chapter 6

Savings and Investment Quotes, http://www.humblesavers.com/quotes/

A Guide To Investing In Cash Alternatives, http://saf.
wellsfargoadvisors.com/emx/dctm/Marketing/Marketing_
Materials/Mutual_Funds/e6509.pdf

Alternative Payments: Cash Alternative Payment Services, http://
www.fraudpractice.com/alt-cash.html

Exchange – Traded Fund – ETF, Investopedia, http://www.
investopedia.com/terms/e/etf.asp

Chamberlain, Michael, *What's The Difference? Mutual Funds and
Exchange Traded Funds Explained,* http://www.forbes.com/sites/
feeonlyplanner/2013/07/18/whats-the-difference-mutual-funds-
and-exchange-traded-funds-explained/

About ETF's, http://www.bloomberg.com/markets/etfs/etf_about.
html

Exchange Traded Funds, https://www6.royalbank.com/
educationcentre/english/alternative-investments/exchange-
traded-funds.html

Learning About Asset Classes – Cash Alternatives, https://www.
retireonline.com/rpsparticipant/education_center/The_Way_
Forward/Learning_about_asset_classes_-_cash_alternatives.jsp

Frequently Asked Questions About Money Market Funds, https://
www.retireonline.com/rpsparticipant/education_center/
The_Way_Forward/Frequently_asked_questions_about_money_
market_funds.jsp

Frequently Asked Questions About Stable Value Funds, https://
www.retireonline.com/rpsparticipant/education_center/The_
Way_Forward/Frequently_asked_questions_about_stable_value_
funds.jsp

Chapter 7

Savings and Investment Quotes, http://www.humblesavers.com/quotes/

What Is a BDC?, http://www.cnlsecurities.com/education/what-is-a-bdc.stml

Investment Options of BDC's, http://www.cnlsecurities.com/education/what-is-a-bdc.stml#options

Why Invest in Non-Traded BDC's, http://www.cnlsecurities.com/education/what-is-a-bdc.stml#why

Evaluating Non-Traded BDC's, http://www.cnlsecurities.com/education/what-is-a-bdc.stml#evaluate

Boyd, J, *Front-End Bonus Payments May Need To be Disclosed,* http://www.pageperry.com/securities/nontraded_business_development/

Non-Traded REIT, Investopedia, http://www.investopedia.com/terms/n/non-traded-reit.asp

Real Estate Investment Trust – REIT, Investopedia, http://www.investopedia.com/terms/r/reit.asp

Black, Michael, *Non-Traded REITs Offer Stability and Portfolio Diversification,* http://www.ccim.com/cire-magazine/articles/non-traded-reits-offer-stability-and-portfolio-diversification

Features and Benefits of Structured Products, https://www.rbcwminternational.com/structured-product-benefits.html

Structured Note, http://www.investopedia.com/terms/s/structurednote.asp

Make Sense of Structured Notes, http://www.moneysense.gov.sg/understanding-financial-products/investments/guides-and-articles/making-sense-of-structured-notes.aspx

Chapter 8

Assets Quotes, Brainyquote, http://www.brainyquote.com/quotes/keywords/assets.html

Adkisson, Jay, *Ten Rules For Asset Protection Planning,* http://www.forbes.com/sites/jayadkisson/2011/07/13/ten-rules-for-asset-protection-planning/

Pagliarini, Robert, *6 Asset Protection Strategies To Shield Your Wealth,* http://www.forbes.com/sites/robertpagliarini/2013/10/09/6-asset-protection-strategies-to-shield-your-wealth/

Asset Protection Planning, http://www.helsell.com/faq/faq-asset-protection-planning/

Garber, Julie, *What Is Asset Protection?,* http://wills.about.com/od/advancedestateplanning/a/assetpro.htm

Chapter 9

Famous Retirement Quotes, Funny Retirement Quotes, Inspirational Retirement Quotes, http://www.newretirement.com/Planning101/Thoughts_On_Retirement.aspx

Estate Planning, http://www.aarp.org/money/estate-planning/

Estate Planning, http://www.investopedia.com/terms/e/estateplanning.asp

Mayoras, Danielle and Andy, *Five Estate Planning Lessons From The Paul Walker Estate,* http://www.forbes.com/sites/trialandheirs/2014/02/10/five-estate-planning-lessons-from-the-paul-walker-estate/

Novack, Janet, *The Forbes Guide To Estate Planning: 2013 Edition,* http://www.forbes.com/sites/janetnovack/2012/10/14/the-forbes-guide-to-estate-planning/

Chapter 10

Social Security Quotes, http://www.brainyquote.com/quotes/keywords/social_security.html

Get Head of Your Estate Planning, http://money.cnn.com/magazines/moneymag/money101/lesson21/

Online Social Security Handbook, http://www.ssa.gov/OP_Home/handbook/handbook.html

Ruffenach, Glenn, *The Baby Boomer's Guide To Social Security*, http://online.wsj.com/news/articles/SB119514459625294332

Kessler, Glen, *Social Security: A Guide To Critical Questions*, http://www.washingtonpost.com/blogs/fact-checker/wp/2014/01/08/social-security-a-guide-to-critical-questions/

Chapter 11

Doyle, Alison, *Retirement Quotes*, http://jobsearch.about.com/od/quotes/a/retirement-quotes.htm

Damato, Karen, *Psst...The Backdoor Route To a Roth IRA*, http://online.wsj.com/news/articles/SB1000142405 27023041045045793754322141266642?mg=reno64-wsj&url=http%3A%2F%2Fonline.wsj.com%2Farticle%2F SB10001424052702304104504579375432214126664.html

Klein, Robert, *Considering a Roth IRA Conversion Before Year-End?*, http://www.marketwatch.com/story/considering-a-roth-ira-conversion-before-year-end-2013-12-05

Roth IRA Conversion Rules, http://www.rothira.com/roth-ira-conversion-rules

Perez, William, *Roth IRA Conversions*, http://taxes.about.com/od/retirementtaxes/a/Roth-IRA-Conversions.htm

McCormally, Kevin, *7 Myths About Roth IRA Conversions,* http://www.kiplinger.com/article/retirement/T046-C000-S002-7-myths-about-roth-ira-conversions.html

Chapter 12

Financial Quotes, http://www.brainyquote.com/quotes/keywords/financial.html

Kaplan, Eve, *Suze Orman's Take on Financial Planners,* http://www.forbes.com/sites/feeonlyplanner/2013/01/25/suze-ormans-take-on-financial-planners/

How To Choose a Financial Planner, http://guides.wsj.com/personal-finance/managing-your-money/how-to-choose-a-financial-planner/

Lerner, Michele, *When Should You Turn To a Financial Advisor For Help?, http://www.dailyfinance.com/2014/02/06/financial-advisor-should-you-hire-one/*

Diamond, Mindy, *Is Your Financial Advisor Independent, An RIA or Wirehouse Rep? You Have No Idea But You Should,* http://www.forbes.com/sites/advisor/2012/08/01/is-your-financial-advisor-independent-an-ria-or-wirehouse-rep-you-have-no-idea-but-you-should/

Touryalai, Halah, *How To Check Out Your Stock Broker,* http://www.forbes.com/sites/investor/2011/07/05/how-to-check-out-your-stock-broker/

How To Check Out Your Broker or Investment Advisor, http://www.nasaa.org/2709/how-to-check-out-your-broker-or-investment-adviser/

Rose, Jeff, *How To Do A Background Check on Your Financial Advisor,* http://www.investorguide.com/article/3336/how-to-do-a-background-check-on-your-financial-advisor/

Dugas, Christine, *What To Look For in a Financial Advisor,* http://usatoday30.usatoday.com/money/perfi/general/2011-04-28-finding-a-financial-adviser_n.htm

Chapter 13

Financial Quotes, Brainyquote, http://www.brainyquote.com/quotes/keywords/financial.html

Shepherd, Aaron, *How To Weed Out a Good Financial Advisor From The Bad,* http://lifehacker.com/5981896/how-to-weed-out-a-good-financial-advisor-from-the-bad

Glasgow, Donna, *Specialization Brings Success,* http://www.insurance-journal.ca/2013/08/19/specialization-brings-success/

How To Pick a Financial Planner, http://www.kiplinger.com/article/credit/T064-C000-S001-how-to-pick-a-financial-planner.html

Snider, Susannah, *6 Things You Must Know About Financial Planners,* http://www.kiplinger.com/article/saving/T023-C000-S002-things-you-must-know-about-financial-planners.html

Kosnett, Jeffrey, *Finding a Financial Planner Who's Right For You,* http://www.kiplinger.com/article/credit/T064-C000-S001-finding-a-financial-planner-who-s-right-for-you.html

Chapter 14

Wood, Robert, *20 Inspirational Quotes... About Taxes,* http://www.forbes.com/sites/robertwood/2013/09/20/20-inspirational-quotes-about-taxes/

Income Tax Deductions, http://taxes.about.com/od/Deductions/

Franco, Jeff, *Ordinary Dividends vs Qualified Divided,* http://wiki.fool.com/Ordinary_Dividends_Vs._Qualified_Dividends

Joseph, Chris, *The Difference Between Qualified and Ordinary Dividends*, http://budgeting.thenest.com/difference-between-qualified-ordinary-dividends-3829.html

Guide To Short-Term vs Long-Term Capital Gains Taxes (Brokerage Accounts etc), https://turbotax.intuit.com/tax-tools/tax-tips/Investments-and-Taxes/Guide-to-Short-term-vs-Long-term-Capital-Gains-Taxes--Brokerage-Accounts--etc--/INF22384.html

Long Term Capital Gain or Loss, http://www.investopedia.com/terms/l/long-term_capital_gain_loss.asp

Waldrop, Sharon, *How To Get The Most Out Of Your health Savings Account,* http://www.forbes.com/sites/nextavenue/2013/08/27/how-to-get-the-most-out-of-your-health-savings-account/

About the Author

Sunwook Jin is a wealth advisor at Redwood Financial Network. He focuses on providing wealth management strategies to affluent soon-to-be-retired and current retirees in the Solon, OH, area and across the country. Together with his partners, he helps affluent clients address their five biggest concerns: preserving their wealth, mitigating taxes, taking care of their heirs, ensuring their assets are not unjustly taken, and charitable giving.

Sunwook founded Redwood Financial Network in 2010. He uses a consultative process to gain a detailed understanding of his clients' deepest values and goals. He then employs customized strategies designed to address each client's unique needs and goals beyond simply investments.

Previously, Sunwook spent 11 years as a financial advisor at Natcity Investments/PNC Investments and Northwestern Mutual Financial Network. In 2013 & 2014, he was awarded a Five Star Wealth Manager* by Five Star Professional, a third-party research firm.

Sunwook served as a treasurer for the Greater Cleveland Korean-American Chamber of Commerce in Cleveland for six years. He also co-founded the **Beat Brain Cancer Foundation** and helped raise significant contributions for the **Preston Robert Tisch Brain Tumor Center at Duke Medical Center** in North Carolina. He is an avid golfer and resides in Macedonia, Ohio, with his wife and son.

Sunwook is a member of **Financial Planning Association** and holds the following professional designations: **CFP® - CERTIFIED FINANCIAL PLANNER™, CMFC® - Chartered Mutual Fund Counselor, CRPC® - Chartered Retirement Planning Counselor, and EA - Enrolled Agent.**

For more information on Sunwook, please visit: **http://tendayfinancialblueprint.com**